For the Love of...
GARLIC

THE COMPLETE GUIDE TO GARLIC CUISINE

VICTORIA RENOUX

COVER DESIGNER: Phaedra Mastrocola • TEXT ILLUSTRATOR: Victoria Renoux
COVER PHOTO: Getty Images, Inc. • EDITOR: Elaine Will Sparber
INTERIOR PHOTOS: © by TheGarlicStore.com. See their website at www.TheGarlicStore.com
TYPESETTER: Gary A. Rosenberg

Square One Publishers
115 Herricks Road • Garden City Park, NY 11040
(516) 535-2010 • (877) 900-BOOK
www.squareonepublishers.com

Library of Congress Cataloging-in-Publication Data

Renoux, Victoria.
For the love of garlic : the complete guide to garlic cuisine / Victoria Renoux.
p. cm.
Includes bibliographical references and index.
ISBN 0-7570-0087-8 (pbk.)
1. Cookery (Garlic) 2. Garlic. I. Title.
TX819.G3R46 2005
641.6'526—dc22

2004006628

Printed in the United States of America

10 9 8 7 6 5 4 3 2 1

Contents

This book is dedicated to my sister, Jackie Wheeler,
who helped me type my first manuscript
many years ago, before I learned how to type.

Preface

Love affairs come and go with the waxing and waning of the moon or the changing of the seasons. Sometimes they are as fleeting as the shifting tides. Occasionally, however, if you are lucky, you may stumble upon a passion of such monumental fervor that it lasts for years, sometimes even for a lifetime. This is the type of love affair that inspires epic novels, causes princes to relinquish their thrones, and tempts priests to give up the cloth.

This is the kind of love I have for garlic—the kind of love that leads you to throw all caution to the wind and ride the waves of fate to wherever they may lead. For the love of garlic, I have traveled to the far corners of the earth, or at least to places like France and Italy. I have risked social rejection and have even given up certain other lovers who did not share in my passion.

When you are very young and inexperienced, your attractions tend to lean towards those with pretty faces and good physiques, such as strawberries and corn. Thinking back, such flings now seem somehow trivial or superficial. Give me strength and character over looks any day. Leading a full and robust life is what makes a lover interesting. It's been years since my first encounter with garlic and I am still experiencing different facets of its personality and hearing new stories of its long and infamous past. Every time I think that I have experienced all the pleasures garlic has to offer, I discover a new one, such as half heads of garlic brushed with olive oil, smothered with summer vegetables, and placed on an outdoor grill.

Developing and putting together the recipes for this book was quite a delight, and although many of the recipes are my old standbys, some I newly created and some I got from friends. My dear friend and fellow artist Louise Hamel once said to me that there are three types of people who buy cookbooks—those who use them, those who intend to use them but don't, and those crazy people like us who read them from cover to cover like novels. Louise provided me with several marvelous recipes for this book. Another recipe provider was Stephen Plotkin. Stephen is my neighbor and the best buddy in the entire world to my dog, Pierrot. Stephen has a cookbook collection to rival my own. Cherie Calbom, friend and coauthor, also contributed some great recipes.

Another person who has been extremely helpful in the research for this book, sending me not only abstracts of scientific studies on garlic but also avocados from his California garden (which go so well with garlic), is Charlie Fox of the Wakunaga Company, which makes Kyolic Aged Garlic Extract. Although I got to know Charlie only on the telephone, I found him to be almost as charming as garlic. Also from California, the garlic capital of the United States, is Donna Metcalfe of Good Scents, an online aromatherapy boutique. Donna shared with me some of her favorite garlic recipes, as well as drawings and instructions she made of how to braid garlic. Last but not least, I would like to thank my adorable husband, Jean Renoux, who will eat just about anything I give him. Jean also happens to have a company, Art and Architectural Tours and Seminars, which conducts tours to some of the most beautiful, culturally rich spots on the planet, where I have had the pleasure of tasting lots of marvelous garlic recipes.

Introduction

There are countless forms of earthly pleasures and innumerable objects onto which we can focus our desires. They range from the quiet pleasures of hearth and home to the more exotic enchantments of faraway lands, lavish surroundings, and beautiful loves. As most of us suspect, and the more adventurous know, danger often lurks behind the allures of passion. This danger, be it to our emotional, financial, spiritual, or physical well being, is not just an element of romantic novels, but is very real, indeed. In my life, I consider myself quite lucky because not only have I had the opportunity to experience the sublime bliss of unabashed passion, I have managed to do so in a totally nondestructive way. In fact, my little obsession seems to have done me quite well.

Like the diaries of writer Anaïs Nin, this book is the chronicle of my passion. In Part One, "The Life and Times of Garlic," I will share with you stories of my beloved. In Chapter 1, "Garlic Through the Ages," we will explore some of the folklore and history surrounding garlic. You will learn how people before me loved garlic and how others have passionately disdained the object of my desires.

In Chapter 2, "From Crop to Plate," we will take a look at what garlic is in the botanical sense and how this deceptively simple bulb goes from being a crop in some farmer's field to a pleasure on your plate. It is in this chapter that you will learn how to choose the freshest and best garlic for all of your culinary needs.

Garlic has definitely lived the life of a rogue, being both loved and hated in almost every culinary tradition. In Chapter 3, "Garlics of the World," you will learn about the characteristics of the many varieties of garlic and discover the origins, when known, of the different types.

Every enjoyment eventually grows shallow when all it has to offer is itself. Take ice cream, for example. Ice cream is quite a delight with the first few bites, but with serious indulgence, it becomes a foe, not a friend. Ice cream can make you fat, raise your cholesterol, and, God forbid, create excess mucus and other unpleasant reactions if you are lactose intolerant. Garlic would never do that to you. In spite of its reputation as a stinker, it is steadfast and true. Although it offers culinary delights that can rival those of any food on this planet, garlic has been used throughout history to cure almost every ill known to man and woman. In Chapter 4, "Garlic and Your Health," we will discuss the healing powers and health benefits attributed to garlic.

In Chapter 5, "Growing Garlic at Home," I will share with you how to raise delicious, gourmet garlic right in your own backyard or balcony. Go ahead and take the risk. It's easier than you might think.

In Part Two of this book, we will indulge in "The Tastes and Pleasures of Garlic." In Chapter 6, "Garlic Tips, Tricks, and Tools," we will discuss cooking techniques you may wish to try and special tools you may wish to own. In Chapter 7, "Cooking With Garlic," the real fun will begin, with luscious, healthful recipes that will allow you to indulge in your own garlic fantasies to your heart's content. What does health have to do with passion? Without health there can be no passion, and with these recipes you can have both.

Following the recipes, you will find a resource list showing where to buy gourmet garlics and garlic lovers' paraphernalia. Then finally, as with all good things, this book must end, but you will take with you some new knowledge, perhaps improved health, and hopefully, a love for this marvelous plant that is affectionately called "the stinking rose."

PART ONE

The Life & Times of Garlic

CHAPTER 1

Garlic Through the **Ages**

The air of Provence was particularly perfumed by the refined essence of this mystically attractive bulb.

—ALEXANDRE DUMAS, FRENCH AUTHOR

A lover with experience and a fascinating past, who has traveled the world, who personifies both sophistication and unpretentious earthiness—this is a fine lover to have. To these qualities add good taste, virility, and youthful zest. What more could you desire? Wealth? There are a few snobs who reject garlic because of its connections to the peasantry and because its wealth cannot be measured in dollars. But garlic comes from an old and illustrious genus, *Allium,* which is part of the lily family. As humble as garlic may be, the lily branch of the family has connections to royalty (the fleur-de-lis) and is revered as a Christian symbol of purity. All the alliums, and garlic in particular, have a solid reputation for providing anyone who appreciates them with health and vitality. This in itself is worthy of love. But for those hot-blooded souls, the free spirits for whom virtue alone does not merit affection, there is just enough of the "bad boy" in garlic to make it irresistibly enticing. In this chapter, we will explore the myth and the history surrounding this fascinating character, allowing you to experience the thrills and the excitement of a life lived to the fullest. The garlic snobs don't know what they are missing.

THE ORIGINS OF GARLIC

Garlic has such an ancient past that no one is sure of its origins. However, we do know that it has traveled the world and that it has done so since the earliest days of human history. Most botanists believe that garlic started out in western Central Asia and southwestern Siberia and traveled east, towards China, and west, towards Europe. Garlic's closest living wild relative is *Allium longicuspis,* which grows in the mountainous area near Afghanistan, centered in Kyrgyzstan, Tajikistan, Turkmenistan, and Uzbekistan. Although we often hear of wild garlic varieties in Europe and the Americas, they are not true garlic (*Allium sativum*), which grows wild only in the area north of Afghanistan. Interestingly, some Chinese texts claim that garlic is a native European plant that migrated eastward.

The exoticness and obscurity of its origins make garlic much more interesting than many other vegetables. Take tomatoes, for example—not that tomatoes are bad. They are actually quite good, especially when paired with garlic. But compared to garlic, they are provincial. Tomatoes started out in South America and didn't really begin to travel until the sixteenth century. They were slow to gain acceptance in Europe, partly because people there thought they were poisonous. In the United States, China, and much of the East, tomatoes were not widely accepted until the twentieth century. Although tomatoes do have their charm, they are a bit jejune when compared to garlic.

Garlic, on the other hand, has probably been cultivated for as long as people have known how to plant crops. Even before agriculture, prehistoric women and children dug up wild garlic, along with other edible bulbs of the lily family. These bulbs could be harvested in the fall and stored for several months. They were a good supplemental energy source to help our ancestors survive the hard winters. In fact, remnants of garlic have been found in cave dwellings that are over 10,000 years old.

The word "garlic" is derived from the old English *gar,* which means "spear," referring to the shape of garlic's leaves. The shape of the garlic plant is also responsible for its renown as an aphrodisiac. According to Rudolph M. Ballentine, MD, author of *Radical Healing* (Harmony Books, 1999), "The mysterious similarity between the organizational pattern of a person who is unwell and that of a leaf or root is the key to the power of natural medicine, and the search for patterns in nature that match conditions observed in sick people is the essence of the science of healing through natural remedies." Stated more simply, when the physical structure of a plant resembles a human condition or body part, the plant is good for healing that condition or body part. Dr. Ballentine uses the example of the tree *Thuja occidentalis,* more commonly known as the arborvitae, which has wart-like berries and is used as a remedy for warts. This theory is called the Doctrine of Signatures. The Doctrine of Signatures was used in some form by the early healers and herbalists of every culture as a guide in selecting remedies. Garlic, with its swollen and elongated floral structure rising from a rooted bulb, is suggestive of a phallus. This may be why garlic, since the earliest of times, has been esteemed as an aphrodisiac.

Garlic, with its phallic shape, has long been celebrated as an aphrodisiac.

GARLIC AND THE ANCIENT CIVILIZATIONS

When we go so far back in history, details are inevitably lost. However, we do know that garlic was present to witness the rise and fall of the greatest cultures of Western antiquity. It participated in the construction of the pyramids, was mentioned in the Bible, ran in the first Olympics, and fought for the Roman Empire.

The Ancient Egyptians

Ancient Egyptian records suggest that garlic provided much-needed strength and stamina for the slave laborers who helped build the Great Pyramid.

Although it is impossible to know all of garlic's past adventures, we are aware that it played an important role in the diets of the ancient Egyptians. Both the rich and the poor reaped the benefits of garlic's generous nature. We have learned this from several different information sources. Art is a major source of historical information, and garlic was immortalized in art for the first time that we know of in ancient Egypt. In a tomb at El-Mahasna, clay sculptures of garlic bulbs were found. This tomb was constructed in 3750 BCE, before the reign of the first Pharaoh. These sculptures were probably intended to give strength in the afterlife to the deceased.

Other information sources from which we have learned about the ancient escapades of garlic are literature, papyrus writings, and tomb and temple texts. The Greek historian Herodotus, who lived around 440 BCE, wrote about the Great Pyramid of Cheops at Giza, which was built around 2900 BCE. He noted that the 100,000 or so laborers who helped construct the pyramid were fueled in large part by onions, garlic, and radishes. Records of the quantities of onions and garlic consumed by these workers were scratched into the stones and used as a way of measuring the labor costs for the project. Fifteen pounds of garlic purchased a healthy male slave in ancient Egypt. It is said that garlic was so important to the ancient Egyptians that when the slaves were deprived of their garlic, they refused to work. In fact, some have speculated that without garlic, there may have been no pyramids. Barley bread and beer were other common foods in Pharaonic Egypt, as were cucumbers, leeks, and lettuce, but garlic was special. It was thought to give the slaves the strength and stamina to accomplish their amazing desert feat. Additional written documentation of garlic in ancient Egypt includes a papyrus that reports that Pharaoh Rameses III distributed great quantities of garlic to the temples.

Archaeology and the discovery of actual remains is another source of historical information, and garlic remnants were found in the famous gold-laden pyramid of the boy king Tutankhamen. King Tutankhamen, who brought peace to his country and died at the age of eighteen, reigned about two thousand years after the tomb at El-Mahasna was constructed. Garlic remnants were also found in the tomb of the architect Kha and his wife, Meryet, built around 1500 BCE. You can visit this tomb at the Egyptological Museum in Turin, Italy, where it has been reassembled. Medical papyri from Dynastic Egypt also mention garlic. The Codex Ebers, a medical text dating from 1500 BCE, includes twenty-two different medical formulas containing garlic. Amazingly, the ancient Egyptians and modern science agree about the use of garlic for certain ailments, such as heart problems and tumors.

The Codex Ebers, a 3,500-year-old medical text, lists twenty-two remedies that contain garlic.

The Ancient Hebrews

Like the Egyptian laborers who built the pyramids, Hebrew workers also relied on garlic for their health and strength, and were not happy when they did not have it. One of the most famous early mentions of garlic is in the Bible. In Numbers 11:6, after the Israelites had been led by Moses out of slavery in Egypt, they complained about the absence of garlic: "We remember the fish, which we did eat in Egypt freely; the cucumbers, and the melons, and the leeks, and the onions, and the garlic: but now our soul is dried away; there is nothing at all, besides this manna before our eyes."

The Talmud includes instructions for using garlic as both food and medicine. It states that garlic warms the body, brightens the face, kills parasites, cures jealousy, and encourages love. The aphrodisiac effect of consuming garlic is why it was recommended as a food, along with fish and beet greens, for Friday night. Friday night, in ancient Hebrew tradition, is the night of the marital bed.

Not all writings about garlic in the Talmud are favorable, however. The Sages considered it a danger to life to eat a peeled clove of garlic left sitting overnight. Peeled, boiled eggs and onions were likewise considered dangerous. One Jewish story relates that when a certain rabbi was giving a lesson, he found it difficult to teach because of the stench of garlic in the room. He asked the offending student to leave.

The Ancient Greeks

In ancient Greece, garlic helped fuel the fires of passion for King Minos (thought to be a son of Zeus) and his wife, Pasiphane, whose sexual desires were a little kinky, to say the least. The queen fell in love with a beautiful white bull. To appease his wife, the king had a contraption built in the form of a life-size, hollow wooden cow that she could hide inside to satisfy her lust with the bull. The resulting union gave birth to the Minotaur, a half man–half bull. This, of course, is only myth, but the actual remains of garlic dating from somewhere between 1850 and 1400 BCE have been excavated at the royal Palace of Knossos on the island of Crete, which was built by King Minos. Minoan sailors probably helped to distribute garlic all along the coasts to other parts of the Mediterranean.

Ancient Greek athletes ate garlic to enhance their performances during the first Olympic games.

Most wealthy ancient Greeks, as passionate as they may have been, did not share my love for garlic, at least not in their food. The stench of garlic on the breath was considered vulgar. Therefore, garlic was used mainly for its medicinal properties, which were well recognized. The most famous of all physicians, Hippocrates (circa 460 to 377 BCE), is known to have prescribed garlic as a laxative and a diuretic, and to treat lung disease and uterine tumors. Aristotle (384 to 322 BCE), who wrote on matters as diverse as philosophy, science, metaphysics, and ethics, also used garlic as a remedy. It was on his list of aphrodisiacs. The athletes of ancient Greece are known to have loved garlic, which they ate as a stimulant to improve their performances during the first Olympic games.

Greek soldiers also considered garlic to be a stimulant, taking it to make themselves more courageous in war. In the old Greek comedy *The Acharnians*, Aristophanes wrote of unruly soldiers "all dosed up with garlic." He also wrote of wives who hid their infidelity by chewing on garlic cloves before their husbands came home. The reasoning was that they would smell so repulsive that their husbands would not suspect their misdeeds.

The ancient Greeks believed that the gods disliked the smell of garlic. At the Temple of Cybele, the elders forbade entrance by anyone who smelled of garlic. As offensive as garlic may have been to the refined sensibilities of the gods and the upper class, it was revered for its ability to keep one from harm. In Homer's time, somewhere between 1159 and 685 BCE, garlic had already developed the reputation of providing protection from witches. It was golden garlic that saved Ulysses in Homer's *Odyssey* from the beautiful witch Circe, who turned his companions into pigs. This reputation as a witch repellent would follow garlic forever. Perhaps this reputation came from the gatherers of hellebore, a plant that now is sometimes called the Christmas rose. This beautiful but narcotic and poisonous plant was used in ancient Greece to purge the demons from unfortunate individuals afflicted with mania. Hellebore gatherers rubbed garlic oil on their bodies to protect themselves from the poisonous roots of the hellebore plant.

Ancient Greek and Roman soldiers considered garlic a stimulant. They ate it in abundance to make them more courageous in war.

The Ancient Romans

The Roman culture developed out of the Greek culture, and Roman soldiers, like the Greeks, ate plenty of garlic. Garlic was known as the vegetable of Mars, the god of war. The Roman poet Virgil (70 BCE) spoke of farm workers eating garlic to maintain their strength. Sailors, too, ate garlic to keep themselves healthy during their long voyages at sea.

Garlic-rich foods were probably sold to working-class citizens from street stalls, which were ancient versions of fast-food restaurants. Ordinary Romans did not have kitchens in their homes. They apparently did not have set meal times either. They ate in the streets while going about their business. Wealthy Romans, on the other hand, were fond of entertaining and served elaborate meals cooked in their homes, but garlic was seldom a guest. It was considered a food for peasants and workers.

Like the Greeks, the Romans prohibited people from entering the Temple of Cybele after eating garlic. The Roman scholar Horace shared the upper-class disdain for garlic and spoke of it as being "more poisonous than hemlock." In his *Odes,* he wrote, "If ever son a parent's aged throat with impious hand has strangled, his food be garlic." When he was in Rome, Horace became ill from eating a sheep's head cooked with garlic. He blamed it on the garlic, not ever considering that the sheep's head may have been the culprit. He wrote to his friend of the experience: "Should you taste such a dish, O sprightly Maeccenas, may your mistress repulse your kisses with her hand and flee far away from you."

In one of the world's oldest surviving cookbooks, a tome written by Apicus, there are no recipes that include garlic. In an epilogue to the book, probably written four hundred years later by Vinidarius, a gourmand, garlic is mentioned in the list of spices, but it is not used in the recipes. Other seasonings in the list include pepper, coriander, lovage, oregano, laurel berries, asafetida, leeks, rue, dill, celery seed, pine nuts, cumin, mint, mustard, chervil, ginger, cardamom, saffron, thyme, caraway, and anise. As you can see, the well-stocked Roman household had a very sophisticated pantry. Vinidarius's including garlic on the list may have indicated that it was starting to gain acceptance.

Pliny the Elder recommended garlic for a variety of ailments, including toothaches, tumors, and epilepsy.

Although the Romans still would not award garlic a medal for popularity, they, like the Greeks before them, used it as a medicine. Pliny the Elder (CE 23 to 79) provided detailed information in his thirty-seven-book encyclopedia of natural sciences about the cultivation, storage, and uses of garlic. "Garlic has powerful properties," he wrote. "Garlic is believed to be serviceable for making a number of medicaments, especially those used in the country." He recommended it for warding off scorpions and serpents. Other uses of garlic suggested by Pliny included roasting it and mixing it with oil for snake bites, mixing it with honey as an ointment for shrew and dog bites, applying it to bruises, taking it with vinegar for toothaches, earaches, hoarseness, worms, tumors, and epilepsy; to induce sleep; to improve circulation, making the skin a ruddier color; and, of course, as an aphrodisiac, especially in combination with wine and coriander. Pliny said that garlic should be planted "when the moon is below the horizon" and gathered "when it is in conjunction."

Dioscorides, a Greek who was the chief physician to Nero's army in the first century CE, wrote a celebrated treatise on herbs. In this famous *Materia Medica,* he prescribed garlic for many of the same ailments as Pliny. Pliny foreshadowed discoveries in modern medicine when he wrote that garlic "clears the arteries and opens the mouths of the veins." Herbalists used his writings as a resource until well into the Renaissance. Dioscorides also recommended garlic as a tonic for baldness.

GARLIC IN EUROPE

As the simple and straightforward style of the Byzantine icons developed into the splendor of the high-Renaissance paintings, garlic continued its journey through history. Garlic was witness to the refinements in art, cuisine, and table manners that took place in Europe during one of the most exciting periods of history. It continued to be both loved and hated; but as you will see, when the darkness of the Great Plagues fell upon the land, it was the garlic lovers who fared the best.

Garlic was among the plants grown by medieval Christian monks, who were the keepers of herbal and medical knowledge.

Medieval Times

Roman troops introduced garlic to northern Europe during their far-reaching crusades, but after the fall of Rome, it was Christian monks who became the keepers of herbal and medical knowledge. The monks tended herb gardens around their monasteries, and garlic was among the plants they grew. Charlemagne (CE 742 to 814), King of the Franks and the first emperor of the Holy Roman Empire, chose garlic to be among the seventy-five plants in the royal gardens. This was quite a compliment for the spice that had been rejected by the ancient Greek and Roman bourgeoisie.

All over Europe, common people began to value garlic for its curative properties. In ninth-century Ireland, an anonymous verse was written about the virtues of garlic as a medicine:

Garlic with May butter
Cureth all disease
Drink of goat's white milk
Take along with these.

Another aristocratic proponent of the virtues of garlic was Robert I, Duke of Normandy. In the eleventh century, he wrote, "Since garlic has the power to save from death, endure it though it gives bad breath."

In England, garlic was, and would continue to be, until the twentieth century, largely frowned upon as food by the upper class. There were a few brazen individuals in medieval England, however, who were great garlic lovers. Twelfth-century writer Alexander Neckham, the Abbot of Cirencester, was one. This interesting character was born on the same night as Richard the Lion-Heart and was raised as his foster brother. The scope of Neckham's interests was outstanding. He was the first Englishman to write about chess, silkworms, and refined medieval cuisine in which garlic was a must. He wrote: "A roast of pork is prepared diligently on a grid, frequently basted, and laid on the grid just as the coals cease to smoke. Let condiments be avoided other than pure garlic or a simple garlic sauce." He also recommended garlic for domestic fowl, hen, and fish. Fish, he said, should be cooked in wine and combined with fine herbs and garlic.

In the fourteenth century, garlic made an appearance in England's first published salad recipe. The recipe comes from a manuscript titled *Forme of Cury.* The word *cury* in the title refers to cookery, not curry. Other ingredients in the salad are parsley, sage, onion, leeks, borage, greens, fennel, cress, rue, rosemary, and purslane. In the same manuscript is a recipe for chicken with grapes and garlic. Today, on the menus of some trendy restaurants, you can find a similar dish.

As always, among the poor in England, garlic was a staple, combined with grains and herbs in thick stews, or pottages. This was a time when access to doctors and medicines was limited, and the peasants seemed to have instinctively known that garlic could save them from illness. For the most part, however, the English upper class was still a stuffy lot. Chaucer, in his *Canterbury Tales,* used garlic to describe the unlikable character of Pardoner, the seller of pardons, when he wrote: "Well loved he garleek, oynons, and eek lekes. And for to drinken storng wyn reed as blood."

In Germany, Saint Hildegard von Bingen (1098 to 1179) had an insightful appreciation of garlic. As a child, Saint Hildegard was frail and sickly, which led her to an interior life filled with visions and devotion to God. From a young age on, she heard voices and had a talent for predicting the future. At the age of eight, she was put under the care of a reclusive nun who lived in a convent. Hildegard was never taught to read or write, but when she was around forty years old, she was ordered to write down her visions, which were believed to come directly from God. With the help of a monk who transcribed for her, she wrote about theology, health, natural history, and medicine. She said that garlic "should be eaten in moderation, lest the blood of a man overheats. In truth, if garlic is forbidden, a man's health and proper strength vanish away; but if it is then mixed with food in due proportion, it will bring back his strength." She said that garlic "ought to be eaten uncooked, because if it is cooked, its strength is lost."

Among Saint Hildegard's recorded visions are instructions for eating garlic in moderation.

By this time, garlic was at home on ships and in peasant's hovels, monasteries, and palaces. Starting in the ninth century, garlic had become a regular guest at the world's first seaside resort spa. Physicians from the Greek, Latin, Arab, and Hebrew traditions had founded the medical school/spa resort in Salerno, Italy, near Naples. Salerno appears to have been amazingly similar to today's holistic health spas. Its philosophy was that "health relies on the moderate use of the air we breathe, food and drink, exercise and repose, sleep and wakefulness, and of the passions of the soul, together being called diet." This practice was called dietetics. In the eleventh century, a woman named Trotula occupied the chair at the medical school. Her most famous work, a book entitled *The Diseases of Women,* used remedies made from herbs (including garlic), spices, and oils. She recommended long convalescences and a positive attitude. Although she authored several books, some scholars dispute that she was a woman or that she even existed. Salerno was world famous until the fourteenth century, but began to fall out of fashion with the new ideas of the Renaissance. It remained open, however, until Napoleon forced it to close in 1811.

The Renaissance

With the Renaissance came new ideas in art, science, and cuisine—and garlic, of course, was there to witness the excitement. The Renaissance began in Italy, and the Italians, who by this time had already embraced garlic, passed their passion on to the French along with their many other new ideas. In France, the liberal use of garlic is not part of the traditional cuisine of every region. Onions are more prevalent in the north. One of the great charms of France is how the countryside, architecture, food, and wine are unique in each region. Within this cultural diversity, one thing of which you can be sure is that wherever you find Roman ruins, you will also find garlic-rich cuisine. In the areas where onions are preferred, the influence is Gaelic. Even after the fall of the Roman Empire, the Italians continued to exert an influence over the French. When Catherine de Medici (1519 to 1589) wed the Dauphin of France, her dowry included the city-state of Florence and the green bean, which was unknown in France. The French quickly developed a liking for the vegetable and included it in the Provençal dish *grand aïoli.*

It is rumored that when King Henri IV was born, a clove of garlic was rubbed on his lips as protection from witches and demons.

Catherine's cousin Marie de Medici also brought her culinary influence to France. The puff pastry, so prized by the French, is attributed to Marie. Marie's husband, King Henri IV, was one of the most famous garlic lovers of all times. It is rumored that he was baptized with a clove of garlic in the water. Others say that when he was born, a clove of garlic was rubbed on his lips to protect him from witches and demons because garlic had been known as a witch repellant since the time of the ancient Greeks. Although dear Henry was one of the more popular kings of France, he was also reputed to eat so much garlic that his breath could fell an ox at twenty paces.

In Italy, the use of garlic reached an all-time high with Beatrice d'Este. Beatrice was the object of sonnets by William Shakespeare and, later, of music by French composer Francis Poulenc. She was a friend of Leonardo da Vinci and other cultural luminaries. Her husband was Sforza, Duke of Milan, one of the most lavish of all the Renaissance princes. As decadent as her love life and lifestyle may have been, she was not selfish. The greatest pleasures enjoyed by the beautiful and talented Beatrice came from sharing. This is documented in a letter from 1491 in which she tells her sister Isabella, who was planning a visit: "I cannot enjoy any pleasure or happiness unless I share it with you. And I must tell you that I have had a whole field of garlic planted for your benefit, so that when you come, we may be able to have plenty of your favorite dishes."

Not everyone in high places accepted garlic in cuisine, however. During the Renaissance, as today, it was hated by people who didn't know a good thing when they smelled it. King Alfonso of Castile hated garlic so much that in 1330, he forbade knights who had eaten garlic from appearing in court or speaking to courtiers for one full month!

During the Renaissance, gardens of medicinal plants called "physic" gardens came into vogue. One of the oldest and most famous of these gardens was in Padua (Padova), Italy. This garden was laid out in 1545 with a geometric design of elegant formality. It consisted of a circle enclosing a square, divided into four quadrants by alleys oriented according to the cardinal points. The plants were grown inside small geometric beds. Garlic was among the "simples" grown in the garden. "Simples" were remedies that could be obtained directly from nature, without further concoction. This gem of landscape architecture is still tended today and is just a short train ride from Venice. Other physic gardens were opened in Pisa in 1545, Zurich in 1560, Bologna in 1568, Leipzig in 1579, Montpelier in 1592, and Paris in 1597. The garden in Paris is now called the Jardin des Plantes and is located at the Natural History Museum in the Latin Quarter, bordering the Seine. If you are in Paris, be sure to visit the garden, which offers a relaxing change of pace from the city's hectic activities. The beautiful garden at Montpelier is also still tended and is located across from the University Medical School.

Garlic was one of the medicinal plants grown in "physic gardens," which came into vogue during the Renaissance.

Until the Renaissance, most herbalists still used Dioscorides as a reference. During the Renaissance, new theories were born, and herbs were classified according to characteristics such as hot, cold, dry, and moist. Garlic was considered to be extremely hot and drying, so it was used with more discrimination. John Gerard, a gardener, herbalist, barber, and surgeon, wrote *Gerard's Herbal,* one of the most famous Renaissance herbals, in 1597. He wrote that garlic "yeeldeth to the body no nourishment at all, it ingendreth naughty and sharpe bloud. Therefore such as are of a hot complexion must especially abstaine from it." However, he did recognize that it is useful against the "bitings of venomous beasts." He also wrote that it protects against the plague as a "preservative against the contagious and pestilent aire." After Gerard's death, Thomas Johnson edited the work, greatly improving its accuracy.

Although the French, Spanish, Italians, and Eastern Europeans embraced garlic with gusto, the English upper crust continued to shun it. Shakespeare wrote of garlic on several occasions and always with a negative connotation. In *Measure for Measure,* Lucio rants: "He would mouth with a beggar, though she smelt of brown bread and garlic: say that I said so. Farewell." Bottom in *A Midsummer Night's Dream* beseeches his fellow actors to "eat no onions, of garlic, for we are to utter sweet breath." Hotspur in *Henry IV* bemoans having to put up with a bore by placing him in the same league with garlic. Shakespeare may have been ahead of his time when it came to literature, but he was obviously lagging when it came to cuisine.

During the time of the Great Plagues, garlic was believed to be a protection against sickness and death.

The Great Plagues

The seventeenth-century English did have the good sense to accept garlic as medicine. Since the staid English have always had their share of eccentrics and freethinkers, occasionally some wise individual would go against the norm and become an avid supporter of garlic. Sir John Harrington (1561 to 1612), an English poet and satirical writer, realized the importance of garlic as a provider of health and a protector against infectious diseases when he wrote a verse for *The English Doctor* (1609) making light of garlic's presumed vices:

Sith garlick then hath power to save from death,
Bear with it though it makes unsavory breath;
And scorn not garlick, like to some that think,
It only makes men wink, and drink and stink.

Unfortunately for garlic, the English disdain of strong smells and unruly behavior caused it to remain disliked by the majority. The diaries of John Evelyn

(1620 to 1706) are one of the principal literary sources of information about life and manners in seventeenth-century England. Evelyn wrote of garlic: "We absolutely forbid it entrance into our Salleting [salads], by reason of its Intolerable Rankness, and which made it so detested of old; that the eating of it was part of the Punishment for such as had committed the horrid'st Crimes. To be sure, 'tis not for Ladies Palats. Nor those who court them."

This stodgy mindset was regrettable because during the Great Plagues, the people who loved garlic were protected and those who did not, often died. Knowledgeable doctors carried garlic in their pockets to protect themselves and their patients. It is said that French priests were able to safely minister to the dying, but English priests fell ill, and I'm sure by now that you can guess why—French priests ate garlic.

One of the most intriguing stories about garlic from this time period involves four thieves in Marseilles, France. These thieves were able to remain healthy while making their living robbing dead and dying plague victims. When finally captured, they were forced to tell how they managed to avoid the plague. Their secret was a concoction of wine vinegar, garlic, and herbs. They wore cotton masks that had been soaked in this mixture and they also rubbed the liquid on their bodies. A version of this vinegar, called Vinaigre des Quatre Voleurs, or Four Thieves Vinegar, can still be purchased in Provence. Besides garlic, the potion includes wormwood, rue, mint, sage, and rosemary, as well as a variety of additional herbs depending on the specific recipe. Today, modern practitioners of witchcraft use Four Thieves Vinegar to protect against the spells of other witches.

Four Thieves Vinegar, a concoction of garlic and herbs, protected French robbers from being infected by their plague-ravaged victims.

As time progressed, garlic continued to be loved as both a food and a medicine by the multitudes, with the only exception continuing to be, of course, the English. In the early eighteenth century, the poet Percy Bysshe Shelley visited his friend Lord Byron in Italy. From Italy, he wrote a letter lamenting the state to which his friend had succumbed: "What do you think: Young women of rank actually eat—you will never guess what—garlick! Our poor friend Lord Byron is quite corrupted by living among these people, and in fact, is going on in a way not worthy of him."

The English held onto this attitude until late in the twentieth century. In France, Spain, Italy, and Eastern Europe, however, the appreciation of garlic in cuisine continued to flourish. Across the Atlantic, in the Americas, garlic had already taken off on the new adventure of conquering another frontier. By the eighteenth century, garlic's American saga was already into full swing as the plant made a name for itself in the New World.

GARLIC IN THE AMERICAS

Garlic seems to have a knack for being in the right place at the right time. As always, it finds itself enmeshed in the major events of the day, such as the discovery of the New World. And although to some, garlic may not seem like a superstar, it never goes unnoticed.

The Sixteenth and Seventeenth Centuries

Garlic first arrived in the Americas with the ships of Christopher Columbus.

Garlic is not indigenous to the Americas. It arrived with the crews of Christopher Columbus's ships. These sailors were probably the first to plant garlic in the New World, on the island of Hispaniola, where they stopped to recuperate from their voyages at sea. The Spanish conquistador Hernando Cortés (1485 to 1547) most likely planted it in Mexico after conquering that land. By the seventeenth century, the Indians of Peru valued garlic above all other European roots.

Further north, Spanish priests and explorers brought garlic to St. Augustine, Florida, and to settlements along the coasts of Georgia and Carolina in the sixteenth century when they established missions there. The Spanish explorers brought a variety of European seeds as gifts for the natives and for their own gardens. In these mission gardens, melons, figs, hazelnuts, oranges, chickpeas, greens, herbs, peas, barley, pomegranates, cucumbers, wine grapes, cabbage, lettuce, and sugarcane were grown. The Spanish also brought the sweet potato of the Caribbean to Florida. By the seventeenth century, the Spanish settlements of the sixteenth century with their lush gardens had been abandoned and the English had taken over.

The English, true to their reputation, did not arrive in America with the intention of creating a *nouvelle* English gastronomy. When the first permanent English colony was established in Jamestown, Virginia, in 1607, there were 105 members and only one was a farmer. Following a period of starvation, the new Americans learned to subsist on native staples such as corn and beans. The bland American diet that resulted, however, was more likely due to the Puritan code of ethics than mere necessity. These first English settlers were Puritans escaping religious persecution, and for them, spicy foods were considered not exactly sinful, but a big, lusty step in that direction. The Puritan New Englanders were said to have blamed their woes in part on the adoption of garlic as a flavoring for their rations. Garlic was a food eaten by the Papist French and Italians and was not for the likes of the righteous and sober Puritans.

The Eighteenth Century

In the eighteenth century, the new North American upper classes had, for a brief, shining moment in American culinary history, quite an elaborate style of cooking, utilizing exotic, Middle Eastern–style spices and complex cooking methods. They used rose water, almonds, currants, and cardamom, as well as garlic. This rich, Early American cuisine was documented in a recipe book written by Martha Washington (1731 to 1802) when she was married to her first husband, Daniel Parke Custis, a wealthy man twenty years her senior. When Martha wrote her now-famous cookbook, she was a young wife in her twenties. We usually think of Martha as the prim First Lady that she became, but as a young woman, she was one of the most popular debutantes in Virginia society. Pretty and quite social, Martha was apparently well acquainted with garlic. Married at eighteen and widowed seven years later, she married George two years after the death of her first husband. Martha was eight months older than George.

During the 1700s, garlic was a popular spice enjoyed by the upper classes of the new North America.

This rich, exotic, plantation cookery style was possible for only the elite few and became virtually forbidden in the years to come. Why? Perhaps it was out of necessity, but more likely, it was the fault of the continuing Puritan influence.

Wild Garlic in America

When the English arrived in America, they brought their antigarlic attitude with them, and it took almost three hundred years for this viewpoint to diminish. The Native Americans, however, were already well on their way to an avid appreciation of garlic before the Europeans hit the scene. Although the Native Americans did not have true garlic (*Allium sativum*) available to them, they did have some of its wild relatives, many of which were also quite good.

One of these memorable relatives was *Allium canadence,* which today is called wild garlic, meadow garlic, or wild shallot. *Allium canadence* grows in the north from New Brunswick to Ontario, southward down to Florida, and as far west as Texas. This plant, although smaller than true garlic, has similar flat leaves and an eight- to ten-inch-tall stalk with white or lavender flowers. It resembles garlic because it has bulbils, also called bulblets, at the end of the flower stalk, among the flowers. Sometimes the plants produce bulbils instead of flowers. Like true garlic, **Allium canadence** can reproduce from its bulbils.

Another wild species of garlic is *Allium tircoccum,* also called ramps, wild leek, or wood allium. In Quebec, it is called *ail des bois,* which means "garlic of the woods." In Quebec, which has long been an enclave of gastronomy in North America, locals go out in early spring to pick this delicacy. It is one of the first plants to appear in the forest after the usual much-too-long winter. Garlic of the woods looks like a little lily, since like all alliums, it is a member of the lily family. You can eat the leaves in salads and use the bulbs either raw or cooked. The locals preserve it in salt brine in small jars.

Today, in Quebec, *Allium tircoccum* has become an endangered species and can no longer be sold. However, it can still be picked in small amounts for personal use. *Allium tircoccum* also grows wild in Appalachia, where it is called ramps, but here, too, it is becoming rare. Therefore, if you find some *Allium tircoccum,* please treat it with respect and make sure to always take only a very small amount so that it can regenerate.

In British Columbia and the northwestern United States, indigenous Americans dined on *Allium douglasi,* also called Douglas onion or wild onion. This plant, which has pale pink, globe-shaped flowers, was named for the Scottish explorer and botanist David Douglas (1799 to 1834). Douglas explored more than 12,000 miles of ground by foot, horseback, or canoe, and had more than 200 plants, including the Douglas fir, named for him.

When Meriwether Lewis and William Clark journeyed across the country between 1804 and 1806, they wrote of an allium thought to be the nodding onion, or *Allium cernum.* Several tribes of Native Americans ate this allium. It has deep pink, bell-shaped flowers atop a short stalk that turn downward, or nod, making the plant look quite elegant. Native Americans used indigenous wild garlic both cooked and uncooked. Raw, it helped to protect them against scurvy.

Wild allium grew prolifically in the Midwest. "Skunk place," or *shika-ko,* was the name the Menominee tribe gave to a certain spot known for its wild garlics. This place is known today as Chicago. Another wild garlic in the Midwest is *Allium ursinum.* This species of wild garlic is not indigenous to North America, but was introduced by European settlers. Although it is edible—and, according to wild-food aficionados, quite delicious—it is considered by most people to be a weed.

Later, in the nineteenth century, Lord Byron, who spent a good deal of time in Italy, blamed the Puritan principle of sobriety for England's inferior food. If the French, who had arrived in the Americas at around the same time as the English, had not been banished to Acadia and Louisiana, both of which have wonderful, garlic-rich cuisines, imagine what American food might have become.

Martha Washington wrote her cookbook for herself and her family, not for publication. The only published cookbooks in America at this time were English. The first published American cookbook was *American Cookery,* released in 1796. However, the author, Amelia Simmons, seems to have been a bit of a prude. She definitely was no lover of garlic and espoused the English attitude of rejecting garlic in food. She wrote, "Garlics, tho' used by the French, are better adapted to the uses of medicines than cookery."

The Nineteenth Century

In 1824, a courageous lady from a grand Virginia plantation family, Mary Randolph, wrote a cookbook called *The Virginia Housewife.* With her book, Mary attempted to bring some sophistication to American cuisine. The book contains some richly spiced recipes and advocates the abundant use of cream, butter, and wine. Heeding the call of practicality, Mary also gives advice on how to make preserves, cure bacon, and create mock turtle soup using a calf's head. Mary was famous for her lavish hospitality until a scandal developed because of her husband's political differences with Thomas Jefferson. The scandal left the couple broke. Mary, being a true southern lady, was not daunted by poverty. She opened a boarding house, the only respectable occupation for a woman of her social class, and her fine cooking continued to gain recognition, which prompted Mary to write her famous book. Mary did not use garlic in many of her recipes, but when she did, she did so with abandon. In her recipe "Beef à la Mode," she uses two whole heads of garlic, quite a risk for a lady of this era to take!

Early American medicine relied on garlic as a widely used herbal remedy.

Garlic's uses in early American medicine were many and varied. From the 1880s until the 1930s, there was a school of medicine called the eclectic school that relied mainly on herbal remedies. John King, one of the main proponents of this school, wrote of garlic in his 1887 *American Dispensatory.* The eclectics used garlic for coughs, catarrh, whooping cough, hoarseness, ear problems, tumors, and worms. Until the twentieth century, garlic was also used in mainstream medicine. In fact, in the official *U.S. Dispensatory,* garlic was recommended for stomach disorders and respiratory complications in as late as 1926. By the end of the nineteenth century, thanks to the burgeoning pharmaceutical industry, the use of garlic and other plants for medicinal purposes fell out of favor. There was, however, a brief revival of appreciation for garlic's antimicrobial power during World War I. Because of a shortage of antibiotics, physicians used garlic on the battlefield to dress soldiers' wounds, earning it the nickname "Russian penicillin."

The Twentieth Century

Until the late nineteenth century, when there was a massive influx of immigrants, the main influence in American cooking was still the English Puritans. In the early twentieth century, when the immigrants began opening restaurants in large cities such as New York and San Francisco, the Anglo-Americans in those cities were introduced to culinary diversity. The rest of us started catching up around the mid-twentieth century. Food writer Waverly Root (1903 to 1982), in his book *Eating in America* (Ecco, 1999), described how garlic gained popularity among America's early-twentieth-century fashion set: "Before I left America to live in Europe in 1927, you were looked down upon if you ate garlic, a food fit only for ditch diggers; when I returned in 1940, you were looked down upon if you didn't eat it. It had become the hall mark of gastronomic sophistication."

"No cook who has attained mastery over her craft ever apologizes for the presence of garlic in her productions."

—Ruth Gottfried, *The Questing Cook*, 1927

Until the latter half of the twentieth century, the love of garlic in the United States was reserved for the sophisticated elite and for poor immigrants who came from such garlic-loving countries as Italy and Greece. With the rest of us, garlic was slow to catch on. In some places, there are still laws—remnants from the past—lingering on the books to remind us of our naïve dislike or distrust of the stinking rose. In Marion, Oregon, ministers are forbidden from eating garlic before delivering a sermon. In Gary, Indiana, it is against the law to enter a public theater or a streetcar within four hours of eating garlic. In Alexandria, Virginia, men are not allowed to make love to their wives with the smell of garlic, onions, or sardines on their breath. No, America's affair with garlic was not love at first sight or a whirlwind fling like that with the Hula Hoop. Neither has it been an all-encompassing obsession like those for television and fast food. It has been careful and measured.

Apart from places such as New York and California, the love of garlic has been slow in the making. It is, however, a love that will be with us for a long, long time. Let me recount my first adventure with garlic, and if you are from anywhere between Idaho and Georgia, you may be able to relate. If not, you will probably find the story rather quaint.

I must confess that my first encounter with garlic was at around the age of eighteen. No, it was not love at first sight, just intrigue, and I suspect that if you were raised in Middle America, your first tryst with garlic may have been similar. Most of us who grew up in the culinary wilderness of America's interior during or before the 1950s—or in extremely provincial places such as my hometown during the 1960s or even the 1970s—were pretty naïve about spices. I don't believe that I am alone when I say that in my childhood home, we had only salt and pepper to spice up our lives. There were a few exceptions, of course, such as cinnamon in apple pies and sage in the Thanksgiving turkey dressing. However, all in all, it was a pretty bland existence.

Then one day, I discovered this little Italian place downtown, off the beaten path, away from the cafeterias, steakhouses, and hamburger joints that made up the local restaurant scene. This restaurant was so tiny that it contained only three or four tables. Each table was covered with a red-and-white-checked tablecloth and was topped with a Chianti bottle stuffed with a dripping candle. For this innocent, down-home girl, there was something exciting, exotic, and almost naughty about that dingy, little hole-in-the-wall. The year was 1969, and it was my first time at that restaurant. I ordered a pizza, and it was so unlike Mama's cornbread, fried potatoes, and beans that I just didn't know what to think. But I definitely wanted more.

"Garlic used as it should be is the soul, the divine essence, of cookery. The cook who can employ it successfully will be found to possess the delicacy of perception, the accuracy of judgment, and the dexterity of hand which go to the formation of a great artist."

—Mrs. W.G. Waters, cookbook author, 1920

Not long afterwards, I moved away from home and began to learn to cook. In the beginning, I was timid. A clove of garlic rubbed around the bottom of a salad bowl was about all the boldness I could muster. Then, little by little, I started taking chances. A feeling of freedom developed deep within, leading me time and time again to new heights of culinary thrills and satisfaction. Meanwhile, I was slowly developing an intimate relationship with garlic.

As I said, it was a little Italian restaurant that introduced me to garlic, and I wouldn't be surprised if many of my readers didn't have a similar first-time experience. Italian restaurants have probably been the single most important influence that brought garlic into the American mainstream. In fact, in early twentieth-century America, garlic was nicknamed "Italian penicillin." So, as you can see, in the twentieth century, we went from being a nation hung up on Puritan morals to one that openly embraced the joys and pleasures of fine cuisine. What was once an innocent infatuation with garlic has now grown into a full-fledged passion.

GARLIC IN ASIA

It is not only the Western world that has had a long-standing love affair with garlic. All over Asia, garlic-laced traditions abound. The only exception is Japan. In fact, if there were a country in Asia that could be compared with England for its dislike of garlic, it would be Japan. The reason for this probably stems from the fact that Japan, because of its geographical isolation, has always based its cuisine on regional ingredients such as fish, soy, sea vegetables, rice, and vegetables. Another reason for Japan's traditional disdain of garlic may be a sense of propriety. The Japanese, like the English, are just too polite to reek. Today, however, a new recklessness prevails and restaurants in some of Japan's larger cities actually specialize in garlic cuisine. In these establishments, you can find such unconventional treats as garlic-and-squid pizza.

Among the Asian countries that have culinary histories long steeped in garlic-seasoned fare is Indonesia. In Indonesian cooking, you will find the staples of rice and noodles combined with such unique ingredients as tempeh (made from fermented soy beans), enormous jack fruit, and garlicky peanut sauce. Vegetables, both cooked and raw, and seafood are also plentiful in this cuisine of multicultural influences. Besides garlic, Indonesian cooking uses ginger, galangal, chilies, shrimp paste, lime juice, and salam leaf. Other melting-pot countries where garlic is at home are Malaysia and Singapore, where sailing ships from Arabia, India, China, and Europe influenced the exotic cuisine. The seasonings used here include onions, chilies, and rhizomes such as fresh turmeric. In Thailand, delicious blends of hot and sweet, and sour and salty are spiced with chili, lemongrass, fish sauce, palm sugar, kaffir lime leaf, and garlic. Although the Thai use many of the same ingredients as their neighbors, they use them with a refinement and elegance that is typically Thai. The fact that Thailand is the only country in Southeast Asia to remain independent during the era of colonization may account for its distinctive cuisine. In Vietnamese cuisine, a liberal use of herbs such as basil and cilantro lends a distinctive freshness. Also used are chilies, lemongrass, and, of course, garlic.

China

More garlic is grown in China than in any other country in the world. In the Shandong Province, where most of this garlic is raised, a reputation for fine garlic-laced cuisine goes back to the days of Confucius, who lived around 550 BCE. Garlic, along with ginger, scallions, soy sauce, vinegar, sugar, sesame oil, and bean paste, is used in different ways in every area of China to help make up the many regional styles. Although garlic is not indigenous to China, it has been loved by the Chinese for so long that it may as well be native. It is thought that garlic was first introduced into the country between 140 and 86 BCE. Garlic's antiquity in China is reflected in its name, *suan,* which is written with one single character. As early as the fifth century CE, garlic's importance as a crop in the Red River Valley was documented and was even written about in an ancient poem celebrating springtime. Tradition plays a large role in the Chinese diet, and the basic traditions of food preparation were already in place 6,000 years ago. In Chinese cooking, raw garlic is often added to cold dishes. Although this must be partly for taste, this healthful practice may also be because the Chinese have long had a sense of garlic's power to kill bacteria. When Marco Polo traveled to China sometime between CE 1254 and 1324, he was perhaps startled by the peasants' use of garlic with raw meat. Whether or not he partook of this delicacy we don't know, but he was impressed enough to write about it.

"Garlic is as good as ten mothers."

—Chinese proverb

In *The Yellow Emperor's Classic of Internal Medicine,* one of the oldest documents in Chinese medicine, it is written that "medicine and food are of the same source." The role of the traditional Chinese doctor is to restore harmony and balance, enabling the body's natural healing to take place. In traditional Chinese medicine, herbs, foods, and even people's constitutions are classified according to one of the "four natures," which are cold, hot, warm, and cool. These natures must be balanced for perfect health. Persons with "hot-natured diseases" can be brought back into balance by taking foods and herbs that have cooling properties. Persons with "cold-natured diseases" can regain balance by taking foods and herbs with heating properties. Garlic, along with ginger and hot pepper, is among the foods with hot properties. These foods are not recommended for persons who become easily overheated or who have symptoms of excess heat such as local inflammation, swelling, rash, skin eruptions, or sores. Other signs of a heat imbalance are a bright red tongue, red face, red eyes, nosebleeds, canker sores, and a rotten smell in the mouth. Persons with signs of coldness benefit from the use of garlic and other heating foods. A person with a cold condition feels cold and stiff, moves with difficulty, and tends to have a pale complexion.

India

In India, the sacred texts of the Vedas, dating from 1700 to 1500 BCE, set the framework for what is broadly known as the Hindu culture. *Ved* is translated to mean "life," and the system of Ayurveda, which came out of the Vedas, literally means "life science." Most of what we know today about Ayurveda comes from the Charaka Samhita texts, which date from the fifth century CE. In the Charaka Samhita, garlic was used medicinally for its diuretic properties and its benefits for the digestive tract. It was also thought to be good for the eyes, act as a heart stimulant, and have antirheumatic qualities. In the Ayurvedic system, garlic has been used for protection from numerous illnesses, such as arteriosclerosis, cholera, colic, dysentery, typhoid, tuberculosis, and other pulmonary problems.

In the Ayurvedic system, garlic has been used as a protection from many illnesses.

The Vedas do not speak quite as favorably of garlic as a food, however. Foods in Ayurveda are classified as *sattvic, rajasic,* or *tamasic. Sattvic* foods traditionally nourish and support health and promote a clear, refined state of mind. *Rajasic* foods have an unsettling influence, and *tamasic* foods have a dulling influence. Both garlic and onions, as well as strong spices, are considered *rajasic* and should be avoided by people desiring a harmonious mind-body experience. This thinking coincides with that of the Buddhists, who rejected garlic, as well as that of the ancient Greeks and Romans, who forbade its entrance into their temples but recommended it for athletes, workers, and soldiers.

Although religious Hindus, Jains, and Buddhist monks avoid garlic, it is nonetheless an important part of Indian cookery, which pounds it into pastes with onions and ginger. These garlicky pastes are added to freshly ground and roasted cardamom, cumin, nutmeg, cinnamon, fennel, and fenugreek. Turmeric, providing color and antioxidants, is often added to these rich spice blends, which are fried in ghee and used to season dal (a dish made from lentils, peas, and/or beans) and vegetables, as well as meats in Muslim households. As in the other Asian countries, these dishes are usually served with rice, and in some regions *roti,* or unleavened wheat bread, is also served.

Garlic, as you can see, has been both loved and hated in Asia, much the same as in the West, and amazingly, it has also been used to treat many of the same ailments. Now, before we leave the life and times of garlic, let's take a look at one of the most bizarre episodes in garlic's history—its role as a provider of protection from witches and vampires.

WITCHES, VAMPIRES, AND GARLIC

As for any great lover, many a tale has been told about the adventures, vices, and virtues of garlic. Some of them we know are true, and about others we will never know for sure. We do know that garlic has long been used for protection and strength. It has been employed throughout history, both by witches and against witches. In the herbals of witchcraft, garlic is considered a powerful substance, and cloves are worn or hung over the threshold as a protection against the evil eye. Some witches believe that garlic, when taken to bed, will induce more vivid dreams. In Belize, it was, and perhaps sometimes still is, used in love potions along with ruda leaves, alcohol, and a few strands of hair and threads from the underwear of the desired lover. A drink of this concoction is supposed to make you irresistible to your beloved.

Inducing love is always a worthy occupation, but there are rumors that garlic has also been involved in black magic. In Belize, you can cause someone harm by having a *brujo,* or witch doctor, make a preparation containing some hair from a black cat, a photograph of the person you wish to harm, sand from a cemetery, and, of course, garlic. I don't know if this works, but some things are best left unknown. For the most part, however, garlic has traditionally been used for good. In the language of flowers, it means "go away, you evil one."

No history of garlic would be complete without a word on vampires, and in vampire lore, garlic has always played the role of protector. Many cultures have vampirelike myths, but the ones with which we are most familiar today are from Eastern Europe. Vampires are the nondead who feed off the blood of the living. Myth has it that they abhor both garlic and sunlight. Once a vampire is among us, it is very difficult to eradicate. Most people's ideas about vampires come from Bram Stoker's 1897 book *Dracula* and the movies that the book inspired. In the pre–Bram Stoker era, however, vampires were usually common folks—peasants living in small villages, not counts wearing black capes and residing in castles.

Garlic has been deemed a powerful substance for thousands of years—which probably explains why it has been used both by witches and against witches!

The Slavic people have the richest vampire lore, and garlic plays an important role. According to vampire legend, there are several possible causes of vampirism—for example, being born with a tooth, a tail, or a caul (part of the amniotic sac covering the head); being conceived on certain days; suffering an irregular death, such as from suicide or falling off a wagon; being excommunicated; or being improperly buried. Witches become vampires after death unless their bodies are properly disposed of. Other potential vampires are children born out of wedlock and children who die before baptism. The seventh child of the same sex in a family is likewise doomed, as is the child of a woman who did not eat salt during her pregnancy. The child of a woman who was looked at by a vampire during her pregnancy is similarly fated. The most classic way in which a person becomes a vampire, however, is to be bitten by one.

You can always tell a vampire is in the neighborhood by the unexplained deaths of animals, especially cattle and sheep. When neighbors mysteriously die, it may also be the work of a vampire. For centuries, corpses were regularly exhumed and examined for signs of vampirism. In the Eastern Orthodox Church, a corpse is considered to be a vampire if it has been buried for a certain length of time and still appears lifelike. This has caused some confusion because in the Roman church, an incorrupt body is the mark of a saint. Other signs of vampirism are the hair or fingernails continuing to grow after death or a body swelled up like a drum. Additional signs are fresh blood in the mouth of a corpse or a ruddy complexion. Holes in the earth around a grave are also a signal that a vampire is buried there. Perhaps the best, or at least the easiest, method for detecting a vampire is to distribute garlic in church. Anyone who will not eat the garlic is more than likely a vampire.

Garlic is said to provide excellent protection against vampires—whether it is placed on windowsills, hung above doorways, or rubbed on doorknobs.

Ways in which people protect themselves from vampires include placing garlic on windowsills and hanging it above doorways. Garlic is also mixed with oil and rubbed on livestock. Other means of protection are mirrors hung on doors, garlic rubbed on doorknobs, and, of course, silver crosses and holy water. A method believed to be excellent for deterring a vampire is to sprinkle millet or other small seeds over the floor. This is because vampires are supposedly such compulsive creatures, they would feel the need to count each seed and thus be, at least temporarily, distracted from their search for fresh blood.

Destroying a vampire is never easy, but there are several traditional methods. One includes placing garlic in the mouth of the corpse. Other, more radical means are wooden stakes through the heart and decapitation, with the head placed between the feet. In the eighteenth century, when vampire scares were at their peak, these methods were actually practiced in remote villages throughout Eastern Europe. Eventually, Austrian Empress Marie Theresa sent her personal physician to investigate the situation. The doctor said that vampires did not exist, and the Empress passed laws prohibiting the opening of graves and the desecration of bodies. This ended the great eighteenth-century vampire epidemic. Today, however, there are still some folks who claim the lifestyle of vampires as their own. These modern-day vampires scoff at some of the ancient superstitions, especially those concerning crosses, holy water, and garlic. In fact, some contemporary vampires, especially Italian ones, claim to like garlic.

Among the many people who have wondered if garlic really does protect against vampires are Nobel Prize laureates Hogne Sandivik and Anders Baebeim, who conducted a satirical scientific study to seek the truth of the matter. Owing to a lack of vampires willing to participate in their study, they substituted leeches. In strictly standardized research surroundings, the leeches were to attach themselves either to a hand smeared with garlic or to a clean hand. The results of the study showed that the leeches, in two out of three cases, preferred the garlic-smeared hand. Therefore, the researchers theorized, the traditional belief that garlic has prophylactic properties against vampires is probably wrong. The reverse may in fact be true. So, to keep vampires out of Norway (where the experiment was conducted), the scientists recommended that restrictions on the use of garlic should be considered.

The above study was done for fun, but the following case illustrates how journalism or pseudoscience can be harmful when it gets out of hand. Several years ago, some articles appeared suggesting that persons suffering from a rare hereditary disease called porphyria were actually vampires, or that persons in the past who were thought to be vampires really suffered from porphyria. Porphyria sufferers do have a certain blood deficiency and are extraordinarily sensitive to sunlight. Garlic purportedly contains a chemical that worsens porphyria, causing sufferers to avoid it, and victims are said to find relief by drinking blood. This theory is completely bogus. Drinking blood does not relieve the symptoms of porphyria and garlic does not adversely affect them, but because of the articles, innocent persons have had to deal with the stigma of being branded vampires.

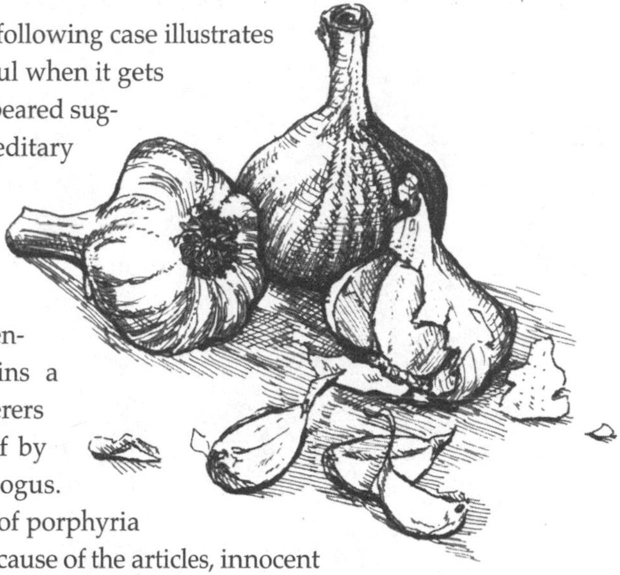

The tales of garlic are abundant and diverse, and amazingly, most are true. Now let's take a look at the journey garlic takes as it's transformed from a humble plant in some rural field to a delight on your plate. We will also discuss how to choose the freshest and the best quality garlic so that you can experience the ultimate in garlic pleasures. Then, we will take a look at just who the garlic lovers out there really are today.

Chapter 2

From **Crop** to **Plate**

Shallots are for babies; onions are for men;
garlic is for heroes.

—ANONYMOUS

The sophisticated world traveler, the provider of health to both peasantry and royalty, the loved, the hated, garlic comes into your home and onto your plate through a rather simple process. In fact, organically grown garlic is raised today much as it has always been. In some cases, it is even still planted and harvested by hand. In this chapter, we will explore how garlic is grown, cultivated, and processed. We will also look at how garlic is marketed.

THE GARLIC PLANT

In the first chapter, we said that garlic is from the illustrious *Allium* genus. This genus comprises more than 600 different species. In the past, garlic's family more commonly was said to be the *Amarylidaceas* family. Today, however, garlic is usually classified as being from the *Alliaceae* family, or lily family. Of the *Alliaceae* family, only about thirty species have been eaten by humans on a regular basis and less than half have been cultivated. The most important are onions (*Allium cepa*), leeks (*Allium porrum*), chives (*Allium schoenoprasum*), shallots (*Allium ascalonicum*), and, of course, *Allium sativum*, the cultivated garlic that we all know and that the sophisticated among us love. Our beloved *Allium sativum* is thought to have evolved from the wild species *Allium longicuspis*. This closest wild relative of garlic grows in an area called the garlic crescent, which runs from the Tien Shan Plateau; across northern Afghanistan, Iran, and the southern Caucasus Mountains; to the Turkish shores of the Black Sea.

Garlic is classified as part of the *Alliaceae* (lily) family.

Garlic plants have long, flat, spear-shaped leaves that usually grow to be sixteen to eighteen inches tall. However, if you measure the flower stalk on the hardneck varieties, some grow up to six feet tall. The garlic plant resembles leeks more than onions or other alliums because of its flat, rather than tubular, leaves. Elephant garlic (*Allium ampeloprasum*) is even closer to leeks than true garlic because elephant garlic and leeks have similar flowers. When garlic "flowers," it produces bulbils at the ends of its flower stalks. Bulbils are small bulbs that are formed in place of true flowers.

When you look at a bulb of garlic, you see the paperlike wrapper that covers the entire bulb as well as each clove. If you take a garlic plant that has been pulled out of the ground, leaves still intact, you will see that the outer wrapper of the bulb forms the older leaves. The younger inner leaves descend into the bulb to surround the cloves. A garlic bulb can consist of as few as three to as many as forty cloves depending on the variety. Each clove has a bud inside that has the potential to produce a new plant.

Garlic is usually divided into two subspecies—*ophioscorodon*, which is called hardneck, or topset, garlic; and *sativum*, which is called softneck, or artichoke garlic. Hardneck garlic produces elongated, woody flower stalks crowned by clusters of curlicued tops called scapes. These scapes have false flowers and up to 150 little bulbils, which resemble miniature green or purple garlic cloves at the end.

The scapes of some varieties grow up to six feet tall, forming loops near the top that make them appear quite dramatic. The bulbils at the ends of the scapes are about the size of a small popcorn kernel. Softneck garlic does not produce bulbils, except in times of stress. Softneck garlic, however, produces larger bulbs and more cloves per bulb. Most of the garlic that we find in supermarkets is of the softneck type because it is more commercially viable, requiring less land and less labor.

WHERE GARLIC GROWS

Although Gilroy, California, prides itself as being the "garlic capital of the world," it is not the world's largest producer. China is the number-one garlic producer,

Elephant Garlic

As those of us who are successful in love know, it does require work. We get out of it what we put into it.

Many wannabe lovers of garlic turn to elephant garlic because peeling and chopping the tiny, tightly wrapped cloves of *Allium sativum* take so much work. They reason that if it looks and smells like garlic, it must be garlic. Wrong!

Elephant garlic (*Allium ampeloprasum*) is actually a relative of the leek. It does look like garlic—gigantic garlic. The bulbs can weigh more than a pound, and a single clove of elephant garlic can grow as large as an entire bulb of true garlic. Elephant garlic also smells like garlic. It even tastes like garlic—or, at least, like a mild version of garlic. However, if you desire the strength of true garlic, you will be disappointed by elephant garlic.

Don't disregard elephant garlic, though. It does have its merits. It can be thinly sliced and served raw in salads. It is also good cooked in dishes that need a mild garlicky taste rather than the pungency of true garlic. However, elephant garlic tends to burn more easily than true garlic when sautéed or grilled, turning from sweet to bitter, so be careful. It also doesn't keep as well as true garlic.

growing 66-percent of the world's output, or 8,574,078 metric tons in 1996. Chinese garlic is less expensive than the American, and according to some American garlic producers, it is often fertilized with toxic sludge. The California growers are not happy with the import of Chinese garlic into the United States because they cannot compete with the Chinese prices and still earn a living. Chinese garlic is less expensive because labor costs are lower in China. The majority of China's output comes from the Shandong Province, which is southeast of Beijing. Korea comes in second in garlic production, and India, third. The United States comes in fourth, with 277,820 metric tons, and is followed by Egypt and Spain.

The garlic-growing capital of the United States is Gilroy, California.

Gilroy, California, is the garlic-growing capital of the United States. Although garlic can be grown almost anywhere in the United States, it likes rich, well-drained soil and full sun, which California has in abundance. California's garlic production is concentrated in its central valley, which encompasses Fresno, Kern, and Monterey counties. A total of 31,000 acres of land is devoted to garlic production in the United States, with 84 to 90 percent of the nation's crop produced around Gilroy. Most of the garlic grown in California is of the softneck variety. Hardneck garlic is more suited to cold climates. Since garlic can grow in many different climates and soil types, there are small farms throughout the United States that grow garlic, mostly for sale to local specialty stores and farmers markets. States that harvest more than 100 acres of garlic include Nevada, Oregon, Washington, and New York. Garlic is also commercially produced in some parts of Canada.

GROWING GARLIC FOR COMMERCE

The process of growing garlic begins with the planting, which is done sometime in the fall or winter depending on the location and the variety of garlic. Cultivated garlic is not grown from seeds, however. About 15 percent of the nation's crop every year is destined to become seed stock, but what garlic growers call seed stock is not actually seeds. It is simply garlic that was planted and harvested to certify a pathogen-free product. In contrast to garlic's ancient reputation as an aphrodisiac, cultivated garlic is propagated asexually because it does not produce seeds. Only wild garlic continues to make seeds, through which it reproduces. There are a few seed-producing wild varieties that are cultivated today, but these are specialty garlics and not what you generally find on the market.

Cultivated garlic is reproduced from cloves, and the new plants are generally referred to as clones. Garlic is a very labor-intensive crop, since much of the work must still be done by hand. It is also a relatively high-risk crop, with some varieties being riskier than others. This is because it is very sensitive to changes in the weather. After preparing the land by deep tilling—and, on organic farms, by adding compost or manure—the first step in planting garlic is to "crack" the bulbs—that is, separate them into cloves. This should not be done more than forty-eight hours before planting or the cloves will begin to dry out and lose their viability.

Garlic is a perennial plant that is grown as an annual.

Garlic is a perennial plant that is grown as an annual. For nongardeners, a perennial plant comes back every year on its own, while an annual has to be newly planted every year. Two different methods are used to grow garlic. The first and most common method is a one-year plan in which the farmer plants cloves and harvests bulbs. The second method is a two-year plan in which the farmer plants bulbils and harvests rounds the first year, then plants rounds and harvests bulbs the second year. Rounds are immature garlic plants, and the ones that are not planted are sold as garlic scallions, which we will discuss more fully on page 44. Regardless of the planting plan, in the North, planting is almost always done in the fall, before the ground freezes. In southern climates, it can be done as late as January. In some temperate climates, garlic can be planted in the early spring if the weather is expected to remain cold enough to provide the required cold period. Most varieties of garlic need a period of cold before they can form bulbs. Experts believe this period is six to eight weeks at a temperature lower than 40 degrees Fahrenheit, but for some strains it can be shorter. In most cases, the garlic remains in the ground through the winter, just like tulips and daffodils. After planting, the cloves or bulbils go through a roughly two-week dormant phase. If the cloves or bulbils receive adequate moisture and the temperature is good, they will then begin to grow long roots through which they can take in nourishment during the winter. The plants do not grow leaves until spring, but when the weather warms up, they grow rapidly. Young garlic plants are day-length sensitive, meaning they need the longer days of summer to generate bulbs. Often, the bulbs begin to form around the time of the summer solstice.

Garlic comes in many shapes, tastes, and varieties.

The term "biological elasticity" is used to describe the way garlic can acclimate to different regions, soils, climates, and cultural practices. It is what causes the same garlic variety grown in different locations to look and taste differently, and sometimes, two varieties of garlic grown on the same land to resemble each other. For example, if a garlic farmer plants a new variety of garlic, in a couple of years the new variety may look and taste like other varieties in the same field. Or, a red garlic may be red in one location but white in another due to differences in the climate and the soil.

Industrial farms usually prefer softneck garlic, since the cloves can be planted upside down because they do not produce scapes. This allows the planting process to be mechanized. Hardneck garlic must still be planted by hand. On most commercial farms, garlic is treated with the fungicide benomyl before planting to reduce rotting. Although garlic is not the most excessively sprayed crop on the market, pesticides are used to control insects and herbicides are used to control weeds. Since garlic is a heavy feeder, needing rich soil, chemical fertilizers are also used.

When garlic is grown organically, insects are controlled with "least-toxic" pesticides, such as those made with ingredients like soap or neem oil. Fungus is controlled by removing any yellowed or misshapen foliage from the fields and taking care not to plant damaged cloves or bulbils. Garlic specialist Ron Engeland, in his book *Growing Great Garlic* (Filaree Productions, 1995), recommends building up the soil over a period of one to two years with animal and green manures before planting garlic. A rich soil also cuts down on the amount of water needed to irrigate the garlic.

Garlic does not compete well with weeds, so weeding is very important. Commercial farmers use herbicides, while organic farmers mulch the new plants with a top dressing of straw or cultivate them by hand or with a tiller. Weeding must be done by hand near the plants, however, because deep tilling can injure the bulbs. Another safe method of weed control is solarization, which uses the heat of the sun. The tilled soil is covered with clear plastic for several weeks during the hottest part of the summer, with the heat that builds up under the plastic killing the weeds and other pathogens. In Europe, some organic farmers use flame weeding—that is, they burn the weeds out.

From planting to harvest, garlic remains in the ground and must be taken care of for approximately ten months, depending on the variety of garlic and the weather conditions. After the autumn planting, winter dormancy, and spring growth period, the garlic is ready for summer harvesting.

HARVESTING GARLIC

For the growers of hardneck garlic, the first harvest is the cutting of the scapes, or flower tops. If a garlic plant is allowed to put its energy into growing scapes, its bulbs will be smaller, so the savvy farmer cuts off the scapes when they are young and tender. This is usually done around June, a few weeks before the bulbs are ready. These scapes are odd-looking delicacies that are usually sold at farmers markets and specialty stores. They can be chopped and used like scallions, and they are good in pesto. Sometimes they are sold as actual flowers to upscale florists who specialize in unconventional bouquets. Garlic scapes are surprisingly potent, with true garlic taste.

The harvesting of garlic bulbs begins around mid July. The timing is very important because garlic doubles in size during its last month of growth. If it is dug up too soon, it will be small and the parchmentlike skin around the cloves will not have formed yet. This immature garlic will not store well. On the other hand, if the farmer waits too long to harvest his crop, the cloves may pop out of their skin when the garlic is pulled out of the ground. Most farmers judge the maturity of garlic by the leaves. When the bulbs are ready, the leaves will start to turn brown and bend towards the ground. Softneck garlics are harvested when four to five leaves are still green.

Garlic cannot be pulled out of the ground if the soil surrounding it has not first been loosened, because the leaves will break off. On small, organic farms, the soil is loosened by digging under the plants with a pitchfork. On large industrial farms and some of the larger organic farms, it is done by mechanically lifting or skimming under the plants with a blade. If the field was mulched, the mechanical method will not work and the garlic must be harvested by hand. The highest quality garlic destined for fresh markets is usually harvested by hand because the outer cloves can be easily damaged by the mechanized method. Garlic that is sold for dehydration or seed stock is almost always harvested mechanically.

Even with mechanical help, garlic still has to be removed from the field by hand and should be immediately sorted and graded to remove any damaged or diseased plants, which can infect the rest of the harvest. On family farms, the small bulbs are usually kept by the farmer for personal use and the medium-size bulbs are sent to market. Most farmers save their largest bulbs for replanting as next year's seed stock. Garlic can be eaten as soon as it comes out of the ground, but if it is stored, it must be properly cured, or dried.

If the garlic was grown in a light soil, it just needs to be brushed off. However, if it was grown in a heavier soil, it may need to be washed. Most growers prefer not to wash garlic bulbs after they have been dug up because washing can invite mold.

CURING GARLIC

Curing, or drying, is usually done by hanging the garlic by the leaves, with the roots still intact, in a barn or other sheltered location. An unused greenhouse is ideal for curing garlic. In areas with little or no summer rain, the harvested garlic is sometimes just laid out in the field in rows, using the leaves from the plants in one row to cover the bulbs of the plants in the next row. Covering the bulbs like this protects them from sunburn. The exact drying time depends on the weather conditions, but garlic should usually hang for at least ten to fourteen days. Sometimes it may take as long as three to four weeks. At this time, the leaves and roots may be clipped off, leaving one-quarter to one-half inch. The garlic is now ready to sell or store.

If the garlic is to be braided, it should be done before it is completely dry and while the leaves are still pliable. Braiding garlic is a good way for small farms to increase the income they receive from their crop. The family usually does the braiding of garlic on small farms, and on larger farms workers do it. Softneck garlic is the type that is commonly braided, as hardneck is almost impossible to braid because it is not pliable. However, the stems of hardneck varieties can be broken or soaked in water to make them flexible enough to braid. For more on braiding garlic, see page 109.

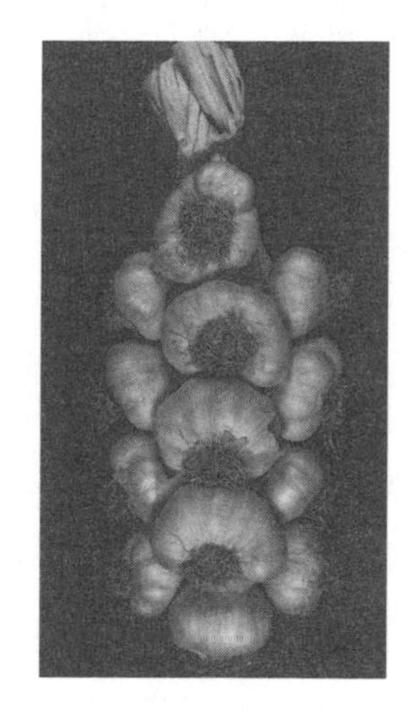

Softneck garlic is the type most commonly braided.

With standard warehouse storage, most fresh garlic varieties will keep for only about three months after harvesting. They will keep for six to eight months when stored at 32 degrees Fahrenheit and at 65- to 70-percent relative humidity. It is important to keep the temperature and humidity constant because any variation in either will induce sprouting or mold. Some garlic varieties can be stored much longer than others, with the longest-storing varieties staying fresh for up to ten months. It is possible to store garlic for about a year in a controlled atmosphere. However, garlic that has been stored for such a long time most likely also has been irradiated or treated with the sprout inhibitor maleic hydrazide.

FINDING FRESH GARLIC YEAR ROUND

There is an off-season in which garlic is scarce in early spring, before the summer harvest. Of course, you can buy irradiated, treated, or imported garlic. You can also use processed garlic or garlic products. But if you want fresh, high-quality garlic, you may need to be creative. Lately, smart farmers have been putting their creativity to work by marketing garlic at various stages of its development. This immature garlic is called green garlic. Selling green garlic extends the farmer's selling season and lengthens the time we can purchase fresh, high-quality garlic.

One way to get fresh garlic before the summer harvest is to buy garlic rounds, or scallions, sometimes also called garlic onions. Remember the two-year planting plan that we discussed earlier in this chapter? This is the method in which the farmer plants cloves or bulbils and harvests rounds the first year. Rounds are immature garlic plants that resemble large scallions because the bulb has not yet been formed. Garlic rounds may look like scallions, but they are garlic and they taste like garlic. They may be slightly milder, but if they were grown from a strong-tasting seed stock, they can be quite potent. If they are picked young enough, the whole plant can be eaten, like a scallion. They can be eaten raw in salads or sautéed in any dish in which you would ordinarily use garlic cloves, which in my opinion is just about any dish you can imagine, except perhaps desserts. As much as I love garlic, I cannot bring myself to embrace garlic ice cream.

Garlic chives are sometimes planted as borders around walkways because they are attractive and grow low to the ground.

Garlic scapes are another way to have fresh, high-quality garlic before the bulbs are ready. Some farmers also grow garlic grass, or green garlic. Although garlic grass is often called garlic chives, it is not true garlic chives (*Allium tuberosum*). Genuine garlic chives are a chivelike plant with flat leaves, pretty round white flowers, and a mild garlic flavor. Garlic chives are sometimes used as border plants around walkways because they are attractive and low growing. Garlic chives are an ingredient in Chinese cooking, where they are called *ku chai* or *gow choy*. The Chinese also use yellow garlic chives, which are just ordinary garlic chives that have been shielded from the sun so that they do not produce chlorophyll. This causes the chives to be yellow. Garlic grass, or green garlic, on the other hand, is simply immature garlic planted close together. It is usually planted from the small, inner cloves of the seed stock, from the cloves of small bulbs, or from bulbils. When it is young, it is as tender as ordinary chives, but a little larger, with flat, bright green leaves and a wonderfully strong garlic flavor. Garlic chives and garlic grass can be snipped with scissors to make a flavorful garnish.

Many of these various forms of garlic can be purchased at farmers markets, on the Internet, or at specialty stores. See page 181 for a list of resources. Garlic grass is especially easy to grow year round in a pot on a sunny windowsill, and garlic in all its stages can be grown in containers or a small garden. See Chapter

5, "Growing Garlic at Home," for instructions. In Chapter 7, "Cooking With Garlic," you will find instructions for cooking with garlic in all of its stages.

GARLIC PRODUCTS

The number of garlic products on the market today is truly amazing. Obviously, the love of my life is getting around. Not only is garlic an ingredient in numerous prepared foods, it is the main feature in more than eighty different food items that I could find—and there probably are many others that I don't even know about! From pickled garlic cloves to garlic-rich salsas, the choice is mind-boggling. So, how does our lovely, earthy friend go from being a bulb curing in some farmer's shed to an ingredient in some gourmet product?

The commercial garlic market in the United States consists of several large shippers, mostly in California, that purchase fresh garlic and distribute it for sale across the country. Garlic that is destined for sale as fresh produce makes up about one-quarter of the entire crop. Great care is taken with this crop to assure that the bulbs have an attractive appearance. Not all garlic destined for the fresh market arrives at the retail stores in the form of bulbs, however. Some of it is used to manufacture crushed, chopped, peeled, or puréed garlic products. There are three or four large firms that process nearly all the dehydrated garlic products available. This equals about 60 percent of the entire crop. Garlic slated for dehydration was planted and harvested to maximize yield, not looks.

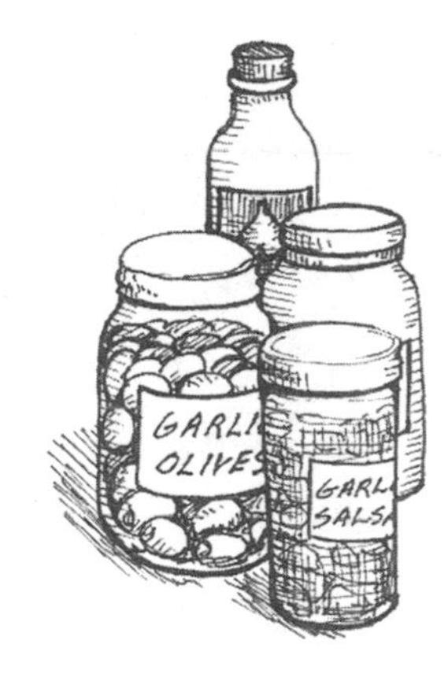

A mind-boggling number of garlic products—from pickled cloves to spicy salsas—are featured in today's marketplace.

Dehydrated garlic is used mainly in processed foods, although a portion of it is used for garlic powders, granules, and salt, which are sold as seasonings. For the true lover of garlic, these seasonings leave much to be desired. There is just no substitute for fresh garlic, and most of us can immediately taste the difference between a dish made with fresh garlic and one made with dried garlic. Dehydrated garlic, however, can come in handy in garlic-lean times or when you are in a hurry, since all you have to do to use it is open the jar and sprinkle.

From what I have been able to discover, garlic powders, salt, and granules contain no additives, although some of the garlic spice mixtures contain xanthan

Who Loves Garlic?

For those of us who love garlic, it is difficult to understand how anyone could not adore a plant of so many virtues. But even though garlic's popularity has grown by leaps and bounds over the last century, it still has its detractors. Today, as in the past, garlic is loved mostly by people of either upper or lower income. Many of us provincial middle-class folk still suffer from some kind of garlic phobia. Roughly 25 percent of all the garlic consumed in the United States is by households with incomes less than 130 percent of the poverty level. This represents 19 percent of the population, which proportionally makes lower-income families greater garlic lovers than any other income group. People earning above 300 percent of the poverty level (49 percent of the population) consume 47 percent of the national garlic supply, which is also more than the average. Men tend to appreciate the stinking rose more than women, consuming 62 percent of all the nation's garlic, and men between the ages of twenty and fifty-nine (27 percent of the population) are the most fervent garlic lovers of all, consuming 41 percent of all the garlic in the United States.

In the last century, we have, fortunately, made some progress away from the dreary Puritan fare of our ancestors. In 1920, when the first estimates of per-capita use of garlic were made, it was found that less than 0.05 pound of garlic was consumed per person per year. Garlic's use rose 25 percent in the 1930s. As we said in Chapter 1, this was due in part to the influx of immigrants and their

gum, maltodextrine, or citric acid. These are pretty innocuous as far as additives go, although citric acid may be genetically modified. Many dehydrated garlic products contain only pure garlic, or garlic and spices with no preservatives whatsoever, which is comforting.

Although most bona fide garlic lovers think of garlic powder as something used by lazy people to make faux garlic bread out of faux Italian loaves, it is an ingredient in some interesting seasoning mixes. In fact, I was surprised to discover how many dehydrated garlic seasonings are available. Some of these are salt-free garlic with spices, garlic salt and parsley, garlic cheese sprinkles, garlic establishment of ethnic restaurants. Other contributing factors were soldiers and travelers who experienced the garlic-rich cuisines of southern Europe, North Africa, and Asia.

In the 1960s, cookbook authors such as James Beard and Julia Child also helped to bring the nation out of its dismal blandness by fearlessly introducing such dishes as garlic chicken with forty cloves. Other garlic missionaries, such as L. John Harris with his self-published books *Garlic Times* and *The Book of Garlic*, also helped to bring our fragrant friend to the mainstream. In the 1990s, garlic's popularity rose like never before, and in 1999, Americans consumed 3.1 pounds of garlic per person. This was partly due to scientific research that showed the health benefits of eating garlic, and to the fact that as people became more familiar with garlic, they just couldn't help but love it.

According to the United States Department of Agriculture's 1994 to 1996 survey of food intakes, 18 percent of Americans consumed at least one food that contained garlic on any given day. This beat both French fries and catsup, which were enjoyed by 13 and 16 percent of the country's population, respectively. Of course, much of this garlic was consumed as an ingredient in processed foods, such as meat dishes, sauces, gravies stews, soups, and dressings. Fast food accounted for 19 percent of garlic consumption, and "better" restaurants accounted for another 15 percent. People who lived in the western states consumed the most garlic. They had 22 percent of the country's population and consumed 31 percent of the garlic. The South and the Midwest were the country's smallest consumers of garlic.

pepper and spices, smoked garlic salt, roasted garlic with sea salt, and garlic pepper that you can grind yourself. You can even find organic garlic powder and garlic granules.

There are some garlic products that will please even die-hard garlic lovers. The most daring of these are whole cloves of pickled garlic, which are sold plain, spicy, or with jalapeños or red chilies. You can even buy organic pickled garlic. There is also Spanish pickled garlic, which, according to the seller, can be "eaten like candy," and pickled whole garlic bulbs. Yes, that's right—*whole* bulbs, not cloves, from Thailand. Other products that appeal to the most ardent of garlic lovers include several varieties of garlic-stuffed olives. These delicious little things are pitted gourmet olives stuffed with whole garlic cloves. You can also find whole garlic cloves preserved in oil with an acidifying agent. Some of the more exotic products are Persian garlic condiments, flavored with lime, lemon, orange, or cinnamon. These can be used for marinating meat, fish, tofu, or tempeh.

If this is not enough, there are garlic hot sauces, some of which are so hot that they come with a warning label and others that claim to be not-so-overwhelming. There are garlic salsas, garlic pasta sauces, garlic pesto sauces, and garlic salad dressings. You may wish to try a pungent spread for your bread such as Caramelized Onion Spread With Garlic, Roasted Garlic and Eggplant Spread, or Olive Tapenade With Garlic, all Garlic Masterpieces made by Dave's Gourmet. These are quite delicious, especially with fresh whole-grain or sourdough bread. Garlic oils, some flavored with basil, thyme, or other herbs, add zest to anything they touch. And let's not forget garlic mustard, one especially delicious variety of which also contains red wine. (There is a plant called the garlic mustard, but it has nothing to do with either garlic or mustard. It is not an indigenous plant in the United States, and because of its prolific nature, it poses a threat to native wildflowers in some parts of the country.)

For some of you more tepid garlic lovers, those who have not yet really made a commitment, fresh minced garlic in a jar is a step up from garlic powder. To me, and to any really passionate garlic lover, one is about as far from fresh garlic as the other. It is another garlic product, however and we are listing garlic products here. You can purchase it, if you are so inclined, but don't expect it to have the same taste in your recipes as fresh garlic. Two new kids on the block of garlic products are garlic juice and roasted garlic juice. These come in spray bottles that claim to have more than 150 cloves worth of juice. However, they just don't have the punch that true garlic lovers desire. One of these juices is made by Cajun Power. It contains garlic, vinegar, and salt and comes in a bottle that allows you to pour it on your food rather than spray it. This helps you to get enough juice on your dish to have some flavor, but it is still not the real thing.

As you can see, comparing garlic products with fresh garlic can become a full-time diversion. In my opinion, the only finer diversion is to taste gourmet varieties of garlic at a garlic festival. Although there are many wonderful garlic products on the market, they just can't compete with fresh garlic used in your own homemade garlic dishes.

CHOOSING GREAT GARLIC

If you are among the passionate garlic-loving souls who decide to go the route of fresh-garlic gastronomy, there are just a few things to consider before taking off. First, what is the best garlic to buy? When you purchase garlic, always take into consideration the season. As you have learned, unless garlic is treated, most varieties will keep for only about six to eight months. Not all garlic varieties are planted at the same time and not all mature at the same time. This adds a few months to the season that high-quality garlic is available. The most "garlicless" season is spring through early summer, after the stores from the summer harvest are gone and before the new harvest is in. So, from May until mid July, you will not find the best garlic. Early spring, however, is the time to find garlic scallions, and by June, the scapes are ready.

Garlic grown in organically certified soil is best.

When you choose fresh garlic, look for firm, heavy, unblemished bulbs with tight skin. The variety you choose is a matter of taste. For a guide, see Chapter 3, "Garlics of the World." Most connoisseurs agree, however, that the hardneck varieties are superior. You can tell a hardneck from a softneck by the hard core that comes out from the center of the bulb to form the stem. Most supermarket varieties are softneck. For hardneck garlic, you will more than likely have to visit a specialty store, health food store, or farmers market. Other ways to buy gourmet hardneck varieties are directly from the growers on the Internet and from mail-order companies. (See the Resource List on page 181.)

When you buy garlic, you are much better off buying organically grown products. Organic produce has not been treated with fungicide, irradiated, treated with a sprout inhibitor, or sprayed with a pesticide or herbicide. The rich soil of organic farms makes for better tasting and more nutritious produce.

Studies have shown that organically grown fruits and vegetables not only contain less harmful pesticide residues, they have a higher content of phytonutrients as well. By buying organic produce, you are helping family farms to earn a living. In many areas, you can buy directly from the farmer, which is a rewarding practice for everyone involved. It allows prices to be lower and gives you and your family a real sense of where your food comes from. Today, most people are amazingly disconnected from the process of farming, while just a few generations ago, the majority of people in this country were farmers. Food is such an essential element of existence, it is frightening to think of how little understanding most of us have of farming and food production. No one wants to eat poisoned or denatured foods, but if we blindly buy what is offered, that is what we usually wind up doing. Buying as much of your food locally, directly from the farmer whenever possible, also helps to create a sense of community in your area. It supports the practice of sustainability that will assure safe food, clean air, and healthful water for future generations.

If you can't find great garlic in your area and don't want to deal with mail-order, you can always grow your own if you have a pioneering spirit. Garlic can be grown on a patio or balcony in a planter box. A suburban back yard can also foster a nice crop. See Chapter 5, "Growing Garlic at Home," for all the information you will need to grow your own great garlic.

Now that you have learned the nitty-gritty of how garlic is grown, harvested, and cured, you must be among the fine ranks of garlic lovers or you would not have come with me this far. So, let's go a step farther and take our pleasure in, passion for, and love of garlic to an even higher realm. In the next chapter, we'll discover some of the world's most wonderful garlic varieties.

CHAPTER 3

Garlics of the World

No one is indifferent to garlic. People either love it or hate it, and most good cooks seem to belong in the first group.

—FAYE LEVY, COOKBOOK AUTHOR

People who love garlic usually do so with the commitment that this grand bulb deserves. They have an ingrained desire to experience every taste and every pleasure that each type of garlic can provide. Yes, there are many different types of garlic, each more exotic and exciting than the last. They offer a whole world of pleasure of which people who don't love garlic don't have an inkling. New garlic lovers, those who are still testing the waters before completely immersing themselves in garlic-drenched ecstasy, may suspect that such pleasures await, but they have probably not yet ventured outside the realm of the two readily available supermarket varieties,

California Early and California Late. People who don't love garlic could care less, but why should we garlic lovers mind? We can smile smugly, aware that what they consider to be stench we know to be ambrosia.

WHICH TYPE OF GARLIC IS BEST?

Which garlic variety is best? You will get as many answers to this question as there are garlic lovers. Everyone has his or her favorites. You may notice that I said "favorites" (plural), not "favorite" (singular), because as far as I know, there is no garlic lover alive who can settle on just one. Garlic lovers are on a never-ending quest for new delights; they are constantly seeking to explore new garlic frontiers. Although the bounty of garlic varieties may seem limitless, most garlic lovers have several favorites from which they pick and choose according to the season, their whims, and how they wish to use the garlic.

I doubt if even the most ardent of garlic lovers has tasted every single garlic variety available, or for that matter, even knows exactly how many varieties exist. One reason for this is the biological elasticity of garlic that we discussed in Chapter 2. If you recall, its biological elasticity allows garlic to change its characteristics according to its location. The same variety of garlic can have different tastes in different fields. The same variety can even taste differently in the same field from one year to the next because of a change in the weather conditions. According to garlic specialist Ron Engeland, there may be more than 450 identifiable strains of garlic. Most of the garlic strains, or subvarieties, however, are just derivations of the basic types and have acquired their specific characteristics because of their local growing conditions.

One thing on which all garlic connoisseurs can agree, however, is that fresh garlic, grown in rich, healthy soil, tastes fuller and more delicious than garlic grown in poor, chemically treated soil. Out-of-season garlic that is kept beyond its prime with the aid of irradiation or sprout inhibitors is also obviously not a garlic gourmand's first choice. All varieties of garlic become stronger and somewhat bitter as they age.

Apart from the question of quality, there are different ways to classify garlic. To help you decide which types of garlic you may wish to try, let's take a systematic look at some of the main types of garlic that are available, starting with hardneck garlic, or *Allium sativum ophioscorodon,* one of the two subspecies into which all garlics are divided. Then we will review some of the groups and varieties within this subspecies. Afterwards, we will look at the other subspecies, softneck garlic, or *Allium sativum sativum,* in the same manner. Before we begin, however, let's go over some of the ways garlic lovers describe the nuances of taste and quality that can be differentiated from garlic to garlic to help you know what to look for when you taste that special clove.

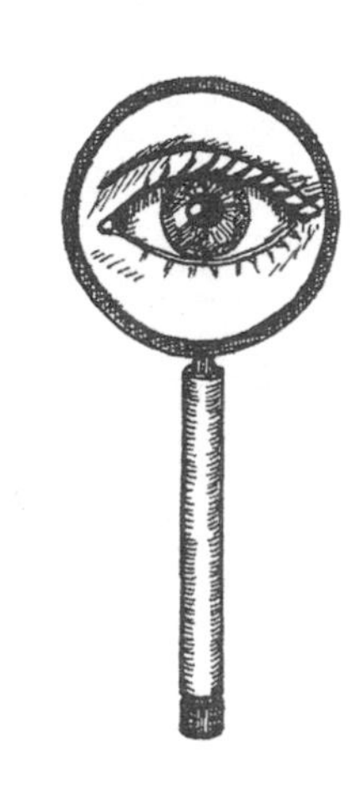

The various tastes of garlic can be characterized by heat, intensity of flavor or "garlickiness," and residual aftertaste.

WHAT TO LOOK FOR

There are different ways of classifying the various tastes of garlic. One is heat. Only raw garlic has the quality of heat, and when people do garlic tastings with roasted garlic, they miss out on this aspect of garlic's character. Not only does the heat of different garlics vary in degree, it also varies in how much time elapses before it's noticeable after a bite is taken. For example, with some types of garlic, the sensation of heat may be delayed by as much as thirty seconds after the bite. Others taste hot immediately. In addition, the time before the heat dissipates also varies among garlics, with some blazing for up to one minute and others cooling off in less than thirty seconds. The degree of heat also varies from a mild, friendly warmth to a raging inferno.

Another taste characteristic for which to look in garlic is the intensity of the flavor, or the "garlickiness." I don't know how else to describe this to you. It has to be experienced, but once you experience it, you will never again settle for garlic of inferior quality. Intensity has nothing to do with heat; there are some extraordinarily flavorful garlics that have only a mild hint of heat, but that have a superb richness that is unique to their variety. After you have tasted a few varieties, you will know exactly what garlickiness is.

The third flavor feature to look for when tasting a variety of garlic is the residual aftertaste. Again, this has nothing to do with the heat. It is a quality that is different from one garlic to another, and once you experience it, you will know what I mean.

These three characteristics can easily be rated from one to ten, with one being extremely mild and ten being extremely strong. One thing you may discover is that everyone has a disparate idea of how the different varieties of garlic taste. Therefore, another characteristic on which you may wish to judge garlic is pure and simple deliciousness according to your own taste buds. This is the best way to discover your personal favorites.

The following listing provides a sampling of the garlics available to help start you on your quest for the perfect clove.

HARDNECK SUBSPECIES

Ophioscorodon garlics, or hardnecks, are often called ophios for short. They are also called topset, stiffneck, or serpent garlic. The terms "stiffneck" and "hardneck" come from the woody, false flower shoot, or scape, that the plant sends up before maturing. The term "serpent" refers to the tendency of the long scape to coil, or form loops. A field of hardneck garlics with their twisting, almost sculptural scapes is quite an impressive sight. Hardnecks are the older type of garlic and are most like the original wild garlics, which today grow only in Central Asia. Hardneck garlic has been cultivated for somewhere between 3,000 and 6,000 years.

Hardneck garlic is usually thought of as northern garlic because it has trouble adapting to warm climates. Although the cloves from a hardneck plant are usually larger than those from a softneck, there are sometimes only four to eight cloves per bulb, with occasionally as few as three or as many as twelve. Hardneck cloves grow in one single, circular layer around the woody stem, and they are of a more uniform size than softneck cloves. The bulb shape is slightly elongated compared to that of the softnecks, which are a little stockier.

Hardneck garlic has some disadvantages that make it less desirable among the large garlic producers than the softneck. A primary disadvantage is that there

A Garlic Tasting Party

After you take the plunge and purchase some exciting and exotic garlic varieties, there is only one way to learn which types you prefer—by tasting them. Just as fine wines, cheeses, and coffees have their special nuances of fragrance and taste, garlic has the same. To the uneducated pallet, there may not be great differences, but when you learn what to look for, you will see very distinctive variations among the garlics. The best way to taste-test garlic is to try several different varieties at the same time so that you can compare them. Just make sure to include all your friends, close relatives, and coworkers in this activity to prevent any social ostracism that you might otherwise have to endure afterwards. With so many people involved, you may as well make it a party—a celebration of the garlic harvest or of anything else that is worthy of such an honor.

The first thing to do when planning a garlic-tasting fête is to choose a date. The appropriate time is anywhere from mid July through November, when fresh garlic is at its peak of flavor, without the strong, bitter taste that develops when it gets old. Arrange to purchase several garlic varieties, from either local growers or mail-order suppliers. Your own garden is another good source. A dozen or so types of garlic is a good variety for an intimate home tasting, being enough to supply some diversity but not too many to cause confusion.

On the day of the tasting, arrange the garlic on your table with labels indicating the variety and any other facts you feel are worthy or interesting. In addition, supply small plates, knives, little bouquets of fresh parsley, fresh baguettes of crusty bread or some whole-grain sourdough loaves, little carafes or shallow bowls of good-quality extra virgin olive oil, and bottled water with glasses.

Separate the garlic bulbs into peeled cloves, and have your guests slice little bits from the cloves. *Note: Do not mince the garlic cloves. Garlic that has been minced loses its strength.* Between tastes, encourage your guests to chew on sprigs of parsley and enjoy the crusty bread that you have provided with some olive oil. You may even wish to provide notebooks so your guests can jot down comments.

After the tasting, serve your guests garlic soup, a salad with a garlic vinaigrette, cheese, and wine. For dessert, try some juicy pears poached in red wine and served with sprigs of fresh mint or a refreshing sorbet.

is less output per acre than for the softneck. The hardneck also requires planting by hand, while softneck can be planted mechanically. Then there is the question of the scape. For the bulb to grow large, the scape needs to be cut, which requires additional labor. Other commercial disadvantages of hardneck garlic are that it doesn't keep as well as softneck and that, although it isn't impossible to braid, its hard, woody scape makes it quite difficult.

In spite of these drawbacks, hardneck varieties are the garlics preferred by most connoisseurs. In fact, some growers call hardneck garlic "gourmet garlic." In the eyes of many a garlic admirer, hardneck is also the more beautiful garlic, with either snowy white bulbs with a satiny sheen or highly colored bulbs in shades of red or purple. According to numerous garlic lovers, hardneck is the better-tasting garlic. Some also say that it has a larger variety of tastes than the softneck. Perhaps the biggest advantage of hardneck garlic for any serious cook is that the hardneck is easier to peel.

Hardneck garlic is divided into three groups—the rocambole group, the porcelain group, and the purple stripe group.

Rocamboles are often celebrated as the best tasting and most desirable of all the garlics.

Rocambole Group

Rocamboles are usually considered northern garlics because they are almost impossible to grow in a southern climate. Many people believe they are the best tasting of all the garlics, with a remarkable richness and depth of flavor. They are the favorite garlics of some of the most knowledgeable of all the garlic connoisseurs, including garlic writer and grower Ron Engeland.

Rocamboles must be enjoyed in their season, which is relatively late. The time of their availability is the shortest of all the garlics because they can be stored for only two to four months. For garlic lovers, this scarcity only adds to their desirability. They are the easiest garlics to peel, making them a favorite with chefs. Rocamboles also have a thinner bulb wrapper than other hardnecks, and although they have a brownish cast that gives them an almost dirty appearance, they have lots of purple streaks and splotches that give them character.

Rocambole cloves are a rich brownish hue and usually number from six to eleven per bulb. Another interesting characteristic of rocamboles is how their scapes form from one to three tight loops and then resume their vertical growth.

Four popular rocambole varieties are the German Red, the Spanish Roja, the Killarney Red, and the Polish Carpathian.

German Red

German Red garlic has a deep, rich red color that is tinged with purple and brown. With an average of eight to twelve easy-to-peel cloves, these large bulbs are said to have come to this country with the German immigrants. Like all the rocamboles, German Red likes cold weather and does not store well. It has a nice, strong, long-lasting flavor that can be described as very hot, rich, and spicy. Harvest time is mid season.

Spanish Roja

Spanish Roja is an aristocrat of the garlic family. In botanical terms, it is considered an heirloom because its lineage can be traced back 100 years or more. Many people use Spanish Roja as the standard when judging true garlic flavor.

Although today it is called Spanish, when it first came to this country, it was known as Greek garlic or Greek blue garlic. The bloodlines of aristocracy can become quite tangled, *n'est-ce pas*?

Anyhow, Spanish Roja has thin bulb wrappers with colors that vary from light brown to teak with lots of purple. The cloves are also brownish, with a strong, hot, and spicy flavor that tends to last. Spanish Roja does not grow well in warm or damp climates. Harvest time is mid season.

Killarney Red

For areas with mild and wet winters, Killarney Red seems to do better than the other rocamboles. However, it does not store well because its bulb wrappers are especially thin.

Killarney Reds are fairly large. In appearance, they resemble German Reds and Spanish Rojas, and are thought to have come from one of the two. The flavor of Killarney's easy-to-peel cloves is very strong and spicy, with a sustained heat and what some people describe as a garlicky-butter aftertaste. Harvest time is mid season, but a little later than the other rocamboles.

Polish Carpathian

Polish Carpathian garlic is a cold-weather garlic from the Carpathian Mountains in southeastern Poland. The plants are rather large, with dark green leaves and tall scapes. Like other rocamboles, this garlic peels easily but does not store well, both due to its thin bulb wrappers. The wrappers have lots of purple and brown, with some reddish orange veins.

Polish Carpathian produces bulbs that are about two and a half inches in diameter. The cloves are a good size, with eight to ten per bulb. This garlic is recommended for pickling because of its rich, zesty flavor and spicy sustained heat. Harvest time is late mid season.

Porcelain Group

Many garlic lovers consider the members of the porcelain group to be the most beautiful of all the garlics. Their tight, thick outer bulb wrappers have a pristine white, reflective sheen, which makes them look as if they were modeled out of fine white porcelain. They have only four to eight cloves per bulb, but the cloves are huge, often as large as an unshelled Brazil nut and sometimes rivaling those of elephant garlic. They separate easily from the bulb and peel effortlessly.

Porcelains have thick outer bulb wrappers with a pristine, reflective sheen that makes them look as if they were modeled out of fine white porcelain.

Because of their thick wrappers, porcelains can sometimes be stored for up to eight months, which is longer than other hardnecks. Less-than-ideal weather will shorten their storage time, however. The plants are very tall, and with their scapes, they can sometimes reach up to six feet.

Four popular porcelain varieties are the Music, the Georgian Crystal, the Georgian Fire, and the Wild Buff.

Music

Music is a very popular, newer variety of garlic that is sometimes called Prussian white. It likes cold weather and grows large and vigorously under the right conditions. The big cloves have a beautiful pink skin, with a medium heat and pleasant aftertaste that sticks around in the back of the mouth. Harvest time is mid to late season.

Georgian Crystal

Georgian Crystal originated in the Republic of Georgia, between the Black Sea and the Aral Seal. The gorgeous, large bulbs are pure white with a satin sheen. The cloves are also large, with only about six per bulb. Georgian Crystal's flavor is mild and some say almost sweet, which makes it ideal for pressing raw into a dish at the last moment. Harvest time is mid to late season.

Georgian Fire

Georgian Fire did not originate down on the farm in the southeastern United States. Like Georgian Crystal, it hails from the Republic of Georgia. It is large, with four to eight robustly flavored cloves per bulb, and is excellent for roasting, which you may prefer doing with this garlic unless you like a sharp bite in your salad. Georgian Fire is light brown to almost white in color, with streaks of purple. Like other garlics in the porcelain group, its harvest time is mid to late season. It will store for six to seven months.

Wild Buff

Although many garlic lovers think of Wild Buff as a type of wild garlic, it was actually developed by the U.S. Department of Agriculture in Beltsville, Maryland. It is an interesting variety of garlic because even though it is cultivated, it is one of the few available garlics that still has a viable seed. It makes up for its rather small size with its punch, which some people say is overpowering. Wild Buff will store for six to seven months. Harvest time is mid to late season.

Purple Stripe Group

A colorful group of garlics, the purple stripes are true to their name, boasting vertical purple stripes that decorate their bulb wrappers. Their coloring can be affected by the weather and growing conditions, so sometimes purple is the predominant color and other times it is white. Most purple stripe bulbs contain five to six cloves, which have a distinctive paper tail. Marbled and glazed subvarieties of the purple stripe are similar, but have thicker bulb wrappers and fewer cloves per bulb. They also have a mottled or glazed appearance rather than a striped appearance.

The plants in the purple stripe group are as distinctive as their bulbs, with leaves that splay out at wide angles and flower stalks that often make 270-degree curls. All the garlics in this group are good roasters and have won taste tests conducted by Rodale, *Sunset* magazine, Martha Stewart, and others.

Four popular purple stripe varieties are the Persian Star, the Siberian, the Brown Tempest, and the Chesnok Red.

Persian Star

One of the stars of the garlic world, Persian Star is an especially beautiful garlic with thick, purple-striped, white bulb wrappers that become more purple closer to the cloves. The cloves have red tips and long, sharp points, and resemble a star when their layers of bulb wrapper are stripped away.

Persian Star garlic is said to have come to the United States in the 1980s from a market or bazaar in Uzbekistan called a *souk.* Uzbekistan is near what is thought to be the birthplace of all garlic. Persian Star has a mild, pleasant flavor. Harvest time is mid season.

Siberian

Siberian garlic, which probably originated in its namesake, Siberia, is both big and beautiful. It is many a garlic lover's favorite, with its thick, white, purple-striped bulb wrappers that become more purple the more layers are stripped away. It has from five to seven enormous cloves covered by reddish brown clove wrappers with pointed tips. The cloves themselves are creamy colored, with an exquisite, not-too-strong flavor. Siberian garlic can be stored for seven to nine months, which is a long time for a hardneck. Harvest time is mid to late season.

Brown Tempest

Brown Tempest has mottled purple wrappers with no stripes and a satiny texture. This heirloom garlic has six to nine rose-tinged cloves covered by light brown skin. It has a strong, fiery flavor that mellows to a buttery aftertaste. It will store for five to six months, which is longer than most hardnecks. Harvest time is mid to late season.

Chesnok Red

From the Republic of Georgia, Chesnok Red is considered a great all-around garlic for roasting and cooking because it holds its shape and flavor. Its bulb wrappers are loose and thin on the outside but become tighter and thicker near the cloves. The bulbs can grow quite large and average six to ten hefty, easy-to-peel white cloves with cranberry-colored streaks and long points. This garlic will store for about six months. Harvest time is mid to late season.

SOFTNECK SUBSPECIES

Softneck garlic, or *Allium sativum sativum,* is a newer occurrence in the garlic world, having evolved from the hardneck. It is a product of centuries of selective breeding by growers. In fact, *sativum* means "domesticated" in Latin. Softneck garlic is sometimes called artichoke garlic because its shape roughly resembles that of an artichoke, or common garlic, and because artichoke garlic is the group of softneck garlics that is most commonly cultivated.

As we said in Chapter 2, softneck garlic is the variety that is preferred by most commercial growers, and the California Early and California Late that we find in the majority of supermarkets are softneck garlics. Softnecks like mild,

Mediterranean-type winters and are especially suited to the California climate, but since they are relatively easy to grow, they can adapt to the cold better than hardnecks can adapt to the heat. Softneck garlics yield higher outputs per acre than hardnecks, and they produce larger plants with larger leaves and bulbs. One of the reasons they have larger bulbs is that they usually do not produce scapes, which leaves the plants more energy to grow the bulbs. Softnecks also have more cloves per bulb than hardnecks, with one bulb having the capacity to produce up to forty cloves. The cloves are arranged in three to five layers, with the largest cloves on the outside and the innermost cloves sometimes too small to be used. Softneck garlic stores better than hardneck and under the right conditions can be kept for up to nine, and occasionally ten, months. It also has a higher soluble solids content, which make it the better type of garlic for roasting.

Another commercial advantage of softneck garlic is that it can be easily braided, allowing farmers to sell their garlic at a premium price if they so choose. Softneck garlics, however, are generally not as colorful as hardnecks, and they don't have the same sheen. Although beauty is in the eye of the beholder and all garlics are attractive to garlic lovers, most feel that softnecks are not quite as pretty as the hardnecks. But then again, it isn't garlic's good looks that attract most of us in the first place.

Softneck garlic is divided into five groups—the artichoke group, the silverskin group, the Creole group, the Asiatic group, and the turban group.

Artichoke Group

When most people think of garlic, they picture artichoke garlics.

Artichoke garlics have lumpy, spreading bulbs that someone once thought resembled an artichoke. They are the type of garlic that most people picture when they think of garlic.

Artichoke garlics are the easiest to grow and do well in warm climates. They are also the most prolific of the garlic plants. The bulbs are very large and produce anywhere from twelve to twenty cloves, with lots of tiny inner cloves that are too small for most people to bother with. Although we are most familiar with the

California Early and California Late varieties, there are many others, offering a wide range of flavors.

Artichoke garlics are sometimes called Italian garlics or red garlics, but they are neither red nor come from Italy. Artichokes store quite well, which is another reason for their commercial success.

Five popular artichoke varieties are the California Early, the California Late, the Inchelium Red, the Simoneti, and the Polish White.

California Early and California Late

California Early and California Late are the famous garlics of Gilroy, California. And although fame is not always reserved for those with the best taste, the vigor and productivity of these garlics make them the darlings of commercial garlic production. They are the lumpy, off-white bulbs that your local supermarkets probably sell. Although many garlic connoisseurs consider these garlics the least interesting of all, when organically grown in rich soil, they can be amazingly flavorful.

When well-raised, both California Early and California Late are excellent all-around garlics for multiple uses. They are wonderful for roasting and have a tight skin, which helps them to store well. The bulb wrapper of California Early has a pinkish tinge. The cloves have a mild, slightly sweet taste and number about twenty per bulb. Harvest time for California Early is early to mid season. For California Late, it is a few weeks later.

Inchelium Red

The origins of Inchelium Red are unknown, but this popular garlic was first discovered on the Colville Native American Reservation, which includes the town of Inchelium, Washington. Inchelium Red is a large garlic, with its bulbs sometimes growing to more than three inches in diameter and containing up to twenty uniform cloves. It has thick bulb wrappers, which helps it to store for up to nine months. It is high in soluble solids, which makes it denser and heavier than most garlics and one of the best for roasting. It won a Rodale Kitchen's garlic tasting award in 1990. Harvest time is mid season, a little later than that for most artichokes.

Simoneti

With a name like Simoneti, you would think that this garlic is Italian. Instead, it hails from the Republic of Georgia, which is a country chock full of garlic varieties and garlic lovers. Simoneti is a big garlic with a pretty, rosy patina. It has large cloves, which makes it a cook's favorite. It is a productive garlic that grows vigorously and is disease-resistant, making it popular with gardeners. Its mellow taste is mild enough to be enjoyed raw. Harvest time is mid season.

Polish White

Although originally from Poland, Polish White is very popular with garlic growers in New York State. It likes cold weather and grows enormous bulbs containing only ten to thirteen large cloves. Although it is called white, its bulb wrapper sometimes has a purple tinge.

Polish White garlic has an initially hot taste with a lot of character, which some people say makes it perfect for sausage. Harvest time is a little earlier in the season than it is for most of the artichoke garlics.

Silverskin Group

Silverskins have white bulbs with a silvery sheen.

When you buy a garlic braid, you can usually, although not always, count on it being a silverskin. Silverskins have white bulbs with a hint of silvery sheen and a clean appearance. Their necks are long and flexible, while at the same time strong enough to be nicely braided. Some growers feel that they are more difficult to grow than artichokes and are more like hardnecks in their needs. They are the longest-lasting garlics and the ones that are harvested the latest, which is a good thing to know when looking for quality garlic to get you through the garlic-lean times of spring and early summer. In fact, some years, the silverskins last until the new harvest comes out of the ground. They have more cloves per bulb than artichokes, but the bulbs are smaller.

Three popular silverskin varieties are the Rose du Var, the Nootka Rose, and the Locati.

Rose du Var

Ooh la la! A true French beauty, Rose du Var garlic has thick white bulb wrappers and creamy colored cloves with purplish red streaks, fiery red backsides, and blushing red elongated tips. The cloves are all large, with no inner cloves, which makes the Rose du Var a chef's favorite. This garlic tastes as bold as it looks, with lots of heat, and it will keep for eight to ten months. Harvest time is late season.

Nootka Rose

Nootka Rose is from the San Juan Islands off Washington State's Olympic Peninsula. It can grow in all the climate zones in the United States.

The Nootka Rose has pure white bulb wrappers with mahogany colored cloves highlighted with red tips and streaks. The bulbs contain as many as thirty-five cloves, arranged in up to five layers. The bulbs are so pretty that when stripped of their bulb wrappers but kept intact, they can be used to make a unique decorative centerpiece for a festive table. The Nootka Rose is a strong-tasting, long-storing garlic that is excellent for braiding. Harvest time is late season.

Locati

Good things come in small packages, and like many good things, Locati garlic hails from Italy—Milan. Locatis are smaller than most silverskins, but the cloves are good-sized; the bulbs store better than some of the larger garlics. The bulb covers are quite white, with a moderate thickness. The thin, elegant looking cloves have a sweet, rosy blush and are hotter than the average softneck. Locatis store well and are excellent for braiding. Harvest time is late season.

Creole Group

A subgroup of the silverskins, the Creole group resembles hardneck garlic in its single-layer clove configuration. These beautiful garlics also have streamlined cloves with elongated tips. Usually, their bulb wrappers are white, but the cloves

The cloves of Creole garlic are a beautiful red or purple color.

are a striking solid red or purple. Unlike hardnecks, however, Creoles do well in warm southern climates. They have a full flavor with a heat that builds in intensity, and they retain their flavor when cooked. Two popular Creole varieties are the Burgundy and the Ajo Rojo.

Burgundy

The name "Burgundy" refers to the color of the garlic, not to the region in France. Even though Burgundy is a softneck garlic, it is, perhaps, one of the most beautiful of all the garlics with its luscious, deep rose bulb wrappers. By peeling the bulb wrapper away, you will discover clove covers that are almost red with subtle stripes of burgundy. Burgundy garlic is not too hot, but it does have a full, rich flavor. It will keep for about seven to eight months. Harvest time is mid to late season.

Ajo Rojo

Ajo Rojo is a Spanish garlic that is similar to Burgundy garlic in almost every way. One of the primary ways it differs is its color, which is a stunning purple. Its color makes its name a little strange because in Spanish, *ajo* is the word for "garlic" and *rojo* is the word for "red." The other primary way it differs is that its bulb wrappers are a little thicker than those of Burgundy. Surprisingly, however, it does not store quite as well as Burgundy, lasting for just six to seven months. Harvest time is mid to late season, the same as Burgundy.

Asiatic Group

The Asiatic garlic strains are genetically softnecks, but they have the large, plump cloves of a hardneck, with the cloves arranged in a single layer around a false flower stalk. The flower stalk of this garlic type, however, is usually short and drooping rather than tall and coiled. The bulbil capsules contain only a few large, purple bulbils. The bulb wrappers are striped or marbled with purple.

Asiatics generally mature a month before all but the turban group of garlics (see page 68). They must be harvested as soon as their leaves begin to brown or the cloves will separate from the bulb. Four popular Asiatic varieties are the Asian Tempest, the Russian Redstreak, the Pyong Vang, and the Japanese.

Asian Tempest

South Korea is the original home of Asian Tempest. The bulb is large and finely striped with a hint of purple. The distinguishing feature of this plant is the beak of the bulbil, or flower pod, which can reach eighteen inches in length. In Korea, this part of the plant is pickled and considered a delicacy. Asian Tempest is not too fussy about climate and will grow well in both mild and cold areas. It has a rich, long-lasting flavor and will keep for four to six months. Harvest time is early season.

Russian Redstreak

Derived from the rocambole, which is a hardneck garlic, Russian Redstreak has many hardneck characteristics, including an occasional scape. Some growers recommend that the scape be cut to allow the bulb to develop to its largest size, while others say that it makes no difference. The Russian Redstreak has an initially sharp and strong taste, which lingers. The bulb is lightly streaked with purple and must be harvested early, before it overly matures, because the bulb wrappers will split open. It stores for six to seven months and can grow almost anywhere in the United States. Harvest time is early season.

Pyong Vang

Pyong Vang garlic hails from North Korea, from near the capital city of Pyongyang. The bulbs average only five to seven pleasant tasting, not-too-hot cloves. These large cloves have long tails and a rosy purple blush. The bulb wrappers are purple striped, and the bulbs keep for three to five months. Harvest time is very early in the season.

Japanese

An unusual garlic, the Japanese was given to Vicky and Frank Giannangelo of Giannangelo Farms Southwest by an elderly man who had given up growing garlic due to his age. The elderly man said he had been given the garlic by a Japanese man. Japanese garlic is very large with three to seven firm, tan-colored cloves, which sometimes grow almost as large as those of elephant garlic. The flower stalk is short, drooping, and somewhat coiled. Its bulbil capsule can grow up to twenty inches long. The flavor of the garlic is pungent, strong, and pleasant. Harvest time is very early in the season, since Japanese garlic matures a little earlier than the other Asiatic varieties.

Turban Group

Turbans, like the Asiatic group, are a softneck garlic but display hardneck characteristics such as poor storage, a bolting flower stalk, and easy-to-peel cloves with a high aromatic flavor and red or purple striping. Also like the Asiatic group, they must be harvested *au point* and not a day late because their bulb wrappers will split open.

Turbans are ambitious garlics, maturing earlier than any other type and taking the shortest period of natural rest before beginning to sprout. A bulbil capsule with a unique turban shape crowns some of the strains. The cloves are arranged in a single layer around the stem, and even though the plants are rather small, the bulbs are of good size. Harvest time can be as early as mid May. Three popular turban varieties include the Chinese Purple, the Tzan, and the Xian.

Chinese Purple

Vivid purple stripes on a white background make the bulb wrappers of Chinese Purple more colorful than those of most other softnecks. This garlic produces a turban-shaped bulbil capsule at the top of the scape. The cloves number about twelve, and their covers are a dark brownish purple. One grower calls this garlic a "Chinese cherry bomb" because of the instant and intense heat it produces upon tasting. If you like strong garlic, this is one for you. The bulbs will store for five to six months. Harvest time is very early in the season.

Chinese Purple is a very strong type of garlic, producing intense heat upon tasting.

Tzan

The large, striped bulbs of Tzan garlic have a purple blush and from eight to eleven plump, light brown cloves. Tzan is from Shandong Province, which is the garlic-growing center of China. The Tzan garlic available in the United States is usually grown in Mexico and marketed as Mexican Red. Its cloves are arranged hardneck-style, in a single layer around the central stem. Harvest time is very early in the season.

Xian

An uncommon bulb from northeastern China, Xian garlic is similar to Tzan, with large cloves and striped bulb wrappers. Although it is not too hot, it has a rich flavor and is one of the favorite garlics of the famous garlic lover Chester Aaron, author of *The Great Garlic Book* (Ten Speed Press, 1997). Harvest time is very early in the season.

Now you have an idea of some of the myriad types of garlic that are available for you to discover. To order some of these beauties and claim them as your own, see the Resource List on page 181. Just be prepared, as for all good things, to wait. Great gourmet garlics can be had only during each variety's natural season, and don't be surprised if some of them are even sold out before the season is over.

In the next chapter, we will take a look at what garlic can do for your health. If garlic's good taste, fascinating history, and botanical beauty are not enough to make a garlic lover out of you, its health benefits are sure to make you fall head over heels.

CHAPTER 4

Garlic and Your Health

In cases of stings and bites by poisonous animals,
garlic acts as a theriac. Applied to the spot bitten by the viper,
or sting of scorpion, it produces successful results.

—MOHAMMED

Haven't we all, at one time or another, loved someone or something that was not good for us? Perhaps it was that certain beautiful—or occasionally, in retrospect, not so beautiful—person who fascinated us much longer than our good sense and well-being deemed reasonable. Maybe it was a fixation of another sort. Most of us would prefer to forget these indiscretions, but as painful as they may be, it is best to remember that when our love—or should I say "lust"—does not support and nurture our higher selves, the outcome can be devastating. The enveloping whirlwind of pleasure that drags us into the dregs of lust and depravity is tempting to embrace, but we should never forget that the price of succumbing to an unwholesome desire is always more dear than we wish to pay.

How many people do you know who yearn incessantly for chocolate or coffee? As an outsider, you may see the effects of these dangerous infatuations better than the poor hapless souls involved. The added pounds the chocolate fiend is forever fighting and the jitters and withdrawal headaches of the coffee addict are all-too-common sights. As pitiful as these symptoms of depravity may be, I must sadly admit that they are, as we all well know, minor consequences—causalities of an innocent sort—when speaking of unsavory loves. Fatal attractions of a more serious nature are unfortunately too horrible to mention.

So, let's now speak of the positive aspects of love. When the object of your desire returns your passion with a nurturing devotion that rises and soars to the peaks of the sublime but never goes over that all-too-precarious edge of no-return, you know your love is true. This blissfully healthy passion, as rare as it may be, is well within your reach and certainly worth seeking out. But, you may say, a love that is so safe is certain to be dull. I must admit that this is likely to be true, but there are exceptions to every rule, and this one precious exception is what this book is all about. Yes, the love of garlic is—unique in the realm of pleasure—safe but never boring. Garlic can be the fascinating provider of both sensuous pleasure and radiant health. What more could you desire? For many people, healthy food is synonymous with insipid food, but garlic, wickedly delicious as it is, is one of the most therapeutic foods we can eat.

As you saw in Chapter 1, garlic has long had a reputation as a healing and health-providing plant. How much of this is true and how much is only folklore? As I did my research on the history of garlic, I was amazed over and over again by the fact that regardless of the place or epoch, garlic has been repeatedly prescribed for certain illnesses. In Chapter 1, I wrote of the earliest mention of garlic's efficacy as a heart medicine, in the ancient Egyptian Codex Ebers. Today, its success as a heart medicament has been confirmed by several studies. Garlic's antibiotic powers, which have also been verified by science, have likewise long been known by folk healers. However, other ancient claims, such as garlic's aphrodisiac powers, have yet to be proven—or unproven, for that matter. Let's now review some folk cures in which garlic is a main ingredient, and you can decide for yourself which ones may have merit.

FOLK CURES USING GARLIC

Grandmothers, eccentric aunts, and village healers have used folk remedies since early history. Although many of these cures have not been proven, others have received some support from science. So just for fun, let's look at several folk cures using garlic. Folk cures are usually considered harmless. However, if you do decide to try a remedy, please consult with your healthcare practitioner first.

Arthritis

Press or chop the cloves from one bulb of garlic into about a half cup of sesame oil and rub small amounts of the mixture onto your sore joints daily. It is best to store this garlic oil in the refrigerator and heat small amounts before you use it. Do not ingest the mixture because botulism bacteria can develop in garlic oil that has been kept for too long. Adding garlic to the diet along with the daily intake of one tablespoon of apple cider vinegar and one teaspoon of honey in a cup of warm water also has many advocates.

Garlic has been used as a folk remedy for asthma in Western, Ayurvedic, and Chinese traditions.

Asthma

In Western, Ayurvedic, and Chinese traditions, garlic has been used for asthma. In Chinese medicine, herbs, foods, and illnesses are classified as either hot or cold. Garlic is used for what traditional Chinese medicine considers asthma of a cold nature. Since garlic has a warming effect, it is not beneficial for asthma of a hot nature. In Ayurvedic medicine, three cloves of garlic boiled in milk are eaten every night to combat asthma.

An asthma treatment recommended by Saint Hildegard consists of drinking

Garlic and Your Animal Friends

If you are a garlic lover who has an animal companion, you may assume that what is good for you is good for your friend. This is not always the case.

According to most veterinarians, neither garlic nor onions should be given to cats because both can lead to damage of the red blood cells. In the long run, this can bring about hemolytic anemia and potentially cause death. Onions are worse for dogs and cats than garlic, but onions and garlic contain some of the same compounds and both can be potentially dangerous. Cats and small dogs are more sensitive than large dogs, who can eat a little more onions before being harmed. However, even the amount of onions found in some jarred baby foods is enough to harm a cat. Baby food is sometimes recommended for sick cats.

Although garlic supplements specifically for pets exist, it would be wise to consult with your veterinarian before giving them to your animal companion. Some experts believe that aged garlic extract is not harmful to pets, but again, check with your vet to be sure.

Avoid sharing garlic with your feline or canine friends. Garlic and onions contain compounds that can be harmful to animals.

a garlic tea. Simmer three cloves of garlic in water for twenty minutes, then strain and sip. Another Western folk remedy is to mix together two peeled and chopped cloves of garlic and a teaspoon each of apple cider vinegar and honey. Eat this mixture in the morning on an empty stomach. It is speculated that this remedy works by stimulating the reflexes that cause the lungs to release fluid, which thins the mucus and enables it to be expelled by the body.

Athlete's Foot

The antifungal qualities of garlic are said to be effective against the fungus that causes athlete's foot. Methods for using garlic to fight this infection include placing freshly crushed garlic on the affected area for one-half hour. Rinse the garlic off with water. Another way to fight athlete's foot with garlic is to rub a broken clove on the fungus, leaving the juice behind. If this fails, soak a cotton washcloth in vinegar and then rub garlic juice on the cloth. Use the soaked cloth to bathe the afflicted area, then rinse the foot with water. In about one week, the fungus should clear up. Perhaps the easiest remedy is to dust your feet daily with garlic powder.

Caution should be taken with all of these remedies, however, because if the skin is broken, the garlic will cause the area to burn. This is said not to be harmful, but it is painful. If the skin is not broken, the garlic may cause blistering, which again is said not to be harmful. If applying the garlic to unbroken skin is painful, wash the area and try again with a diluted mixture or with garlic oil.

Burns and Blisters

Rubbing a little garlic oil on a burn or blister can bring relief.

Some people have obtained relief from minor burns by gently rubbing garlic oil from a capsule onto the burned area. The same remedy is said to work for blisters caused by ill-fitting shoes. Do not use raw garlic on burns or blisters because it can cause more irritation. Use only garlic oil on burns, and then only on minor burns.

Colds and Flu

The antibiotic and antiviral properties of garlic make it a popular remedy for colds and flu. The next time you have a cold, try garlic oil. Place about one-third cup of olive oil in a blender with several cloves of garlic and process until smooth. Take a teaspoon of this mixture every hour or two. Keep the mixture refrigerated, and discard it after two to three days.

Digestion

Although some people find raw garlic hard to digest, many herbalists prescribe it to aid digestion. Garlic is thought to help overcome the overgrowth of *Candida albicans.* It is also used to kill intestinal parasites. In Ayurvedic medicine, garlic is important as a digestive herb because it stimulates the movement of the intestines

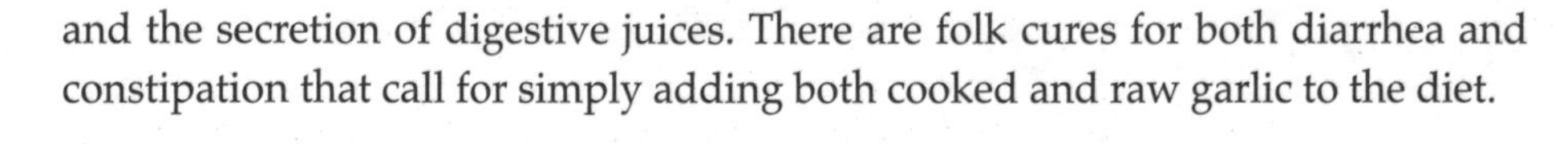

and the secretion of digestive juices. There are folk cures for both diarrhea and constipation that call for simply adding both cooked and raw garlic to the diet.

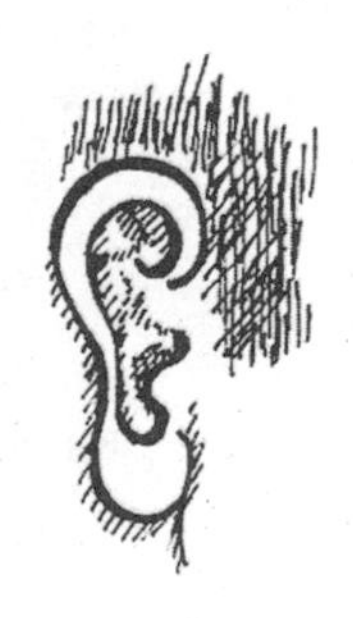

Using garlic oil to cure an earache is an old folk remedy that is still used today

Earache

When I had a health food store in a small village in Quebec, Canada, many of my clients used garlic oil for their children's earaches. There are a few different ways to do this. The easiest is just to pierce a garlic oil capsule and dribble a few drops into the ear. Fresh garlic is probably more effective, however. To use fresh garlic, press a clove into one to two tablespoons of olive oil, then strain the oil through cheesecloth. With the patient lying on his or her side, fill the infected ear with oil. Make a compress using a hot, wet washcloth and hold this over the ear for about fifteen minutes. Make sure to reheat the cloth when it cools. Another method is to place the garlic oil on a piece of cotton and place the cotton in the ear.

Ringworm

Ringworm is a very contagious infection caused by a fungus called tinea; it is not caused by a worm. It is especially common in children and can be found on the scalp, nails, or skin. Because of its antifungal properties, garlic is said to be an effective remedy. To treat ringworm, mix pressed garlic with a little sesame oil and apply three times a day to the affected area.

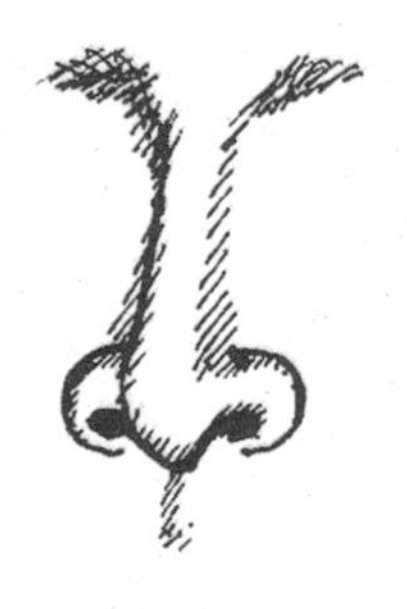

Inhaling garlic from a pouch worn around the neck was once a popular remedy for relieving sinusitis..

Sinusitis

To relieve sinusitis, an old folk remedy is to make a garlic pouch. This remedy doubles as a fashion statement. Fill an old sock, preferably one that has lost its mate, with garlic. Secure it with a shoestring and then tie the ends of the shoestring together so you can wear the sock around your neck. I recommend slightly crushing the garlic for the best results. Wear a garlic pouch whenever you suffer from hay fever, and make sure to color coordinate the sock with your outfit!

Some herbalists recommend using garlic oil as nasal drops. Or, press one clove of garlic and mix with one teaspoon of water and one teaspoon of cider vinegar. Strain the mixture through cheesecloth and drop into the nostrils three times daily.

Sore Throat

To soothe a sore throat, try garlic-ginger tea. Place one cup of water in a small saucepan. Add two cloves of slightly crushed garlic and two to three slices of ginger. Cover the pan and let the mixture steep for ten minutes. Strain the liquid and drink warm.

Another remedy for sore throats is to eat raw garlic along with some food. Do not chew the raw garlic alone, because this will irritate rather than relieve your sore throat.

A traditional Russian folk remedy for toothaches involves applying raw garlic on the wrist.

Toothache

To relieve a toothache, try the following Russian folk remedy—or, as they say in Russia, "grandmother's" remedy. Place pressed raw garlic on the inside of the wrist that is opposite the sore tooth—that is, on the right wrist if the toothache is on the left side of the mouth and on the left wrist if the toothache is on the right side of the mouth. Leave the garlic on the wrist for twenty minutes. It is also said that a cut clove of garlic applied directly to the tooth for about forty minutes will give good results.

WHAT'S IN GARLIC?

When Hippocrates said, "Let food be thy medicine and medicine be thy food," he was perhaps not only reflecting the intuitive wisdom of ancient healers, but foreshadowing discoveries of the very distant future. Unfortunately, during most of the twentieth century, the common-sense wisdom of Hippocrates and other sages was almost forgotten by Western medicine. It was only in 1988 that the U.S. Surgeon General finally acknowledged the value of a good diet in regard to health. According to Paul Pitchford in his book *Healing With Whole Foods* (North Atlantic Books, 2002):

> Food acts as a foundation medicine. It is sometimes slower to take effect, but more profoundly affects all systems of the body. If diet is used correctly for prevention and treatment, other medicines are required less, if at all.

To determine the cause of its many therapeutic benefits, garlic has undergone extensive scientific research over the years.

Pitchford's book, which examines both traditional Oriental medicine and Western nutrition, is used as a nutrition textbook in many acupuncture schools.

In the past few years, researchers have come up with certain foods that they call "functional foods," or "nutriceuticals." These are foods or food ingredients that may provide a health benefit beyond those of the traditional nutrients they contain. There are also commercial products that are called functional foods by their manufacturers, but we are talking only about whole foods in their natural form. Some common foods that are being touted as functional foods are citrus fruits, soy, tomatoes, cruciferous vegetables, flax, and, of course, garlic. Because garlic has been thought over the centuries to have so many therapeutic benefits, it has become a very popular plant to study, with more than 2,500 scientific articles evaluating its health effects.

Trying to discover just what it is in garlic or any food that provides its therapeutic benefits is an enormous task. The chemical composition of all natural foods is extremely complex, and attempts to isolate individual substances that are as effective as the whole food are not always successful. Nature's innate balance of beneficial elements as found in whole, minimally processed foods is still far superior to anything we can fabricate in a laboratory. Garlic is a food remedy that can be described as pleiotropic—that is, it acts in more than one way on the body, and the synergy of its various actions causes its medicinal effects. Garlic contains numerous chemical compounds (some of my sources say up to 200), including vitamins A and C, potassium, phosphorus, selenium, and at least thirty-three sulfur compounds, some of which are water-soluble and others of which are oily. Garlic contains more sulfur compounds than onions or any of the other alliums. It also contains several enzymes and seventeen amino acids. Although no one knows for sure what gives garlic all its healing properties, the principal active components are thought to be several complex sulfur-containing compounds called thiosuphanates. These also give garlic its characteristic odor. Garlic's sulfur compounds are rapidly absorbed, transformed, and metabolized. According to garlic specialist Eric Block, PhD, these sulfur compounds are very fragile and can disappear or change into other compounds depending on how the garlic is processed. This adds to the difficulties in discovering just how garlic actually works its magic.

An unpeeled, undamaged clove of garlic has no odor!

Allin (pronounced *al-lean*) is the stable, odorless derivative of the natural sulfur-rich amino acid cysteine, which is found in garlic that has not been cut or broken. The next time you are about to chop some garlic, take a sniff of an unpeeled clove and you may be surprised to find that there is no odor. Cut or crush the clove and note how an odor is immediately apparent. This is because when you damage a clove, it frees an enzyme called allinase, which transforms the allin and other cystein compounds. These transformed cystein compounds are called intermediates. Little is known about garlic's intermediates because they disappear in about twenty seconds, which is almost as quickly as they appear, and they cannot be stored. The joining together of these intermediates forms another unstable compound, which gives garlic its typical flavor and aroma. This latter compound, called allicin (pronounced *alice-in*), was first chemically isolated in the 1940s. It is only one of several chemical relatives that are created when garlic is cut, but it makes up from 70 to 80 percent of its thiosulphates. It has antimicrobial effects against many viruses, bacteria, fungi, and parasites. Allicin is not as unstable as the intermediates that compose it, but it dissipates within a few minutes of cooking or after a few hours at room temperature.

When crushed or chopped garlic sits at room temperature for a few hours, more stable products are formed. When it marinates in oil, additional compounds are formed. These compounds that are derived from garlic macerating, or breaking down, in oil are called ajoene (pronounced *ah-hoe-ene*), methyl ajoene, and vinyldithiins (pronounced *vinyl-di-thigh-eins*). They were discovered in 1984 by Dr. Block. Ajoene, methyl ajoene, and vinyldithiins are so stable that they can be stored at room temperature for more than a year and are among the most active compounds formed from fresh garlic.

Another sulfur component is produced when garlic is distilled by steam or heated in water. This product is called the distilled oil of garlic, and its major component is diallyl disulfide. Distilled oil of garlic is used in processed food for flavoring. Although garlic's sulfur compounds are thought to be the most active elements in garlic, they are not the only compounds that make it therapeutic. Another major class of compounds in garlic's makeup is a group of soaplike elements called saponins. Saponins also appear to be bioactive, as some of them bind with cholesterol and may be at least partly responsible for garlic's reputed cholesterol-lowering effect. The selenium in garlic also adds to its virtues. Although the selenium is not especially concentrated, it is highly bioavailable and is thought by some researchers to be one of garlic's antioxidant and cancer-preventive components.

As you can see, biochemists have unraveled much of garlic's mystery, but they still do not have our charmingly elusive friend totally figured out. In addition to the changing qualities of garlic's numerous chemical compounds, there are also the questions about the different varieties of garlic and about the biological elasticity that we discussed in Chapter 2. Remember how the same variety of garlic grown in different locations can taste differently depending on the growing conditions, and how different varieties grown together can taste and look similar? This, of course, makes for variations in garlic's chemical makeup. As you continue to read about garlic's medicinal properties, there is one important thing that every garlic lover would want you to remember: Although it appears to have a myriad of wonderfully therapeutic benefits, garlic is food, so eat it!

WHICH FORM OF GARLIC IS BEST?

Everyone wants to know which form of garlic is the most beneficial. Is raw garlic best, and does cooking destroy its valuable properties? Do garlic supplements work, and if so, which supplements are best? As with all questions concerning garlic, there are no simple, cut-and-dry answers. It is difficult to say which form of garlic is best because it changes so dramatically depending on how it is processed. Furthermore, garlic processed by different methods serves different functions. It is possible to say, however, that all forms of garlic are good and for different reasons. So, let's take a look at the different ways you can consume garlic and discuss their advantages and their disadvantages.

Fresh Raw Garlic

The most studied compound in garlic is allicin, which is one of the factors that give garlic its characteristic pungent aroma and potent antibiotic qualities. Allicin is found in fresh raw garlic, and it's the first compound that is unleashed immediately after garlic is chopped or mashed. Allicin does not last for a long time, however, because garlic's enzymatic action transforms it into other compounds. Therefore, to receive the benefits of allicin, you must eat raw garlic fairly soon after it has been chopped or pressed. Cooking destroys allicin. For this reason, capsules and other forms of processed garlic may not be as effective as fresh raw garlic.

Allicin is a compound that contributes to garlic's pungent aroma and potent antibiotic qualities.

But raw garlic can create problems. According to Dr. Block, raw garlic, when eaten alone, can be very irritating and has the potential to injure the digestive tract. For this reason, contrary to some folk remedies, Dr. Block does not recommend eating raw garlic unless it is first processed in oil, such as added to salad dressing or mixed with other foods. When raw garlic is macerated in oil, ajoene, methyl ajoene, and dithiins are formed after the allicin dissipates. These more stable compounds, as well as other sulfur compounds, contained in garlic also are thought to have numerous health benefits. Some of these benefits include anticlotting and antitumor activity. They also have significant antifungal properties and act as antioxidants. When raw garlic is mixed with oil or other foods, it can usually be eaten in moderation without problems. Just remember that garlic is a strong and, according to Oriental healing traditions, very warming food that does have the potential, in certain persons, to cause indigestion and other stomach upsets.

In a study by Mazhar N. Malik reported on *Science News Online* in April 1997, garlic was found to contain about 0.015 international unit of vitamin E per gram. This was roughly 100 times more than had been reported previously. The type of vitamin E, however, depended on whether the garlic was fresh, had been safely aged under refrigeration, or had been extracted from commercial garlic supplements. In fresh garlic, the vitamin E consisted almost exclusively of alphatocopherol, which is the form of vitamin E found in most supplements. There was almost no alpha form E in the garlic pills that were analyzed and no detectable alpha in the aged garlic. In the garlic pills and the aged garlic, the researchers found mostly delta or gamma tocopherol, which are types of E that the body appears to use differently from the alpha form. This research is another illustration of how the various forms of garlic have different chemical compositions and different benefits.

Cooked Garlic

According to some people, when garlic is cooked, it becomes useless because its allicin content is destroyed. It is true that cooking garlic destroys the allicin, but the loss causes other, more stable sulfur compounds to be created. According to David D. Ku, PhD, a pharmacologist and researcher at Pennsylvania State University, it is not necessarily the allicin per se that is garlic's most therapeutic ingredient, but the fact that the string of chemical reactions that takes place when garlic is crushed would not be possible without allicin. The dependence of these other sulphur compounds on allicin is what makes allicin important. Among the sulfur-based allicin derivatives that withstand cooking are S-allyl cysteine (SAC) and diallyl disulfide (DADS), which are thought to possess anticancer benefits. When garlic is cooked whole, however, such as by being roasted in the skin, these compounds are not formed because, since the garlic was not cut, the allicin was not given a chance to form. In a study conducted by John Milner, PhD, of Pennsylvania State University, rats fed garlic cooked in the peel did not benefit from garlic's cancer-preventing qualities. According to both Dr. Milner and Dr. Ku, if garlic is peeled, chopped, and then allowed to set for ten to fifteen minutes before cooking, the anticancer agents SAC and DADS will form. Therefore, when you cook garlic, chop it and then wait ten to fifteen minutes before cooking it to get the most anticancer benefits.

In order to maximize garlic's anticancer benefits, peel or chop your garlic and wait ten to fifteen minutes before cooking it.

Garlic Tablets

Garlic tablets are not all the same. For example, the active compounds in garlic tablets can vary from one brand to the next. If fresh garlic that is to be dried is ground and dried too quickly, the allicin level will be low and the resulting pill will be less effective. If the fresh garlic is ground and dried too slowly, the compounds in the garlic may also be altered. Some companies make garlic pills with a coating that is said to keep the allicin levels of the garlic high.

Garlic tablets were shown to be more effective than garlic oil at improving the blood lipid levels in patients with mildly elevated cholesterol in a 1998 study reported in the *Journal of the American Medical Association*. Deodorized pills, however, are probably less effective because garlic's power in reducing blood lipid levels likely comes from its strong-smelling sulfur compounds. Garlic tablets have also been shown to be more effective at reducing cholesterol than garlic powder used in cooking.

Garlic Oil

There are two ways to make garlic oil. One method involves mashing fresh garlic in a vat and forcing steam through it. The oily compounds rise with the steam and are collected after the steam has cooled. The other method is simply to make a macerate of garlic by combining mashed garlic with vegetable oil. The oil from the garlic joins the vegetable oil, and the garlic solids are filtered out. Both these types of garlic oil are good. Garlic products prepared by steam distillation are rich in diallyl sulfides, while garlic products prepared by oil maceration are rich

in ajoene. These are two different compounds, and as you have seen, the different compounds in garlic all have their special benefits and functions.

In a study reported in the *American Journal of Clinical Nutrition* in 1981, rabbits were fed a high-fat diet and given garlic oil. The garlic oil increased the rabbits' clot-dissipation activity by about 10 percent.

Some people prefer taking garlic supplements to eating garlic because they believe the supplements are odor free, but this is not necessarily true. The various sulfur compounds in garlic oil may be absorbed and then released through the pores. Garlic oil has also been known to cause gastrointestinal distress in some persons.

Aged Garlic Extract

The process for making aged garlic extract has been used by the Chinese for thousands of years. It involves placing sliced garlic in a diluted alcohol solution for a period of up to twenty months. During this time, the chemical composition of the garlic changes, and the chemicals that cause irritation and bad breath are converted to what is said to be more bioavailable, harmless compounds.

Kyolic brand garlic extract is the most popular—and the most thoroughly researched—garlic product on the market.

Research has shown the benefits of aged garlic extract to include cardio protection, liver protection, and immune enhancement. Aged garlic extract has also been shown to have antioxidant benefits and to be helpful in cancer prevention. It has been shown to have antifungal properties and to be effective in certain intestinal conditions. In addition, it has shown effectiveness in heavy metal detoxification, treating herpes, metabolizing sugar, and treating Candida. It has shown promise in fighting Alzheimer's disease and depression.

Aged garlic extract relies for its potency not on allicin, but on water-soluble sulfur-containing compounds. Kyolic, which is a popular brand-name aged garlic extract, is standardized according to its content of SAC, which is not available in oils or tablets made of dry garlic. There have been more than 225 research studies done on Kyolic alone, which makes it the most thoroughly researched garlic product on the market.

By now you may be wondering if there are any disadvantages to aged garlic extract. In a 1984 study published in *Treatment and New Medicine,* Dr. A. Miyoshi found that the long-term use of aged garlic extract caused no serious side effects. This study included more than 1,000 human subjects.

Freeze-Dried Garlic

When garlic is freeze-dried from freshly harvested garlic bulbs, the resulting garlic powder still has the potential to form allicin. This is important because, as was mentioned earlier, allicin is unstable. If the allicin is not preserved, the garlic will be less potent because the allicin is necessary for the creation of garlic's other beneficial compounds. In freeze-dried garlic, the allicin is not activated until water is added. This creates a form of garlic that retains fresh garlic's antimicrobial nature. Freeze-dried garlic capsules with a protective coating that breaks down only in the intestines is the best form of freeze-dried garlic because garlic, to be optimally effective, must be delivered to the intestines with the allicin in the form of its stable precursor.

HOW DOES GARLIC AFFECT YOUR HEALTH?

As a garlic lover, I tend to accept as true every study or article that sings the praises of garlic's health benefits. However, in spite of the many studies that confirm garlic's health benefits, I have found others disclaiming them. Which are we to believe?

I certainly can't tell you which studies are the most reputable. I can only cite some of the more interesting findings, deciphering them from my perspective as a garlic lover. There are books and articles on garlic's health benefits written by scientists and medical doctors, and they also tend to reflect the opinions of their authors. Pat Kendall, PhD, RD, food science and human nutrition specialist from Colorado State University's Cooperative Extension, wrote in 2002, "Although [garlic] remedies sound like folklore, modern science provides evidence to back up garlic's claim to fame."

As anyone who has done research of medical studies knows, it is possible to find a study to prove or disprove almost any point you wish to make. To be able to make truly objective decisions, it would be necessary either to have been personally involved in the studies or to at least know who funded the studies. Pharmaceutical companies may do studies negating garlic's benefits, and garlic-supplement manufacturers may do studies showing its effectiveness. Not that there are no unbiased studies, but how do we know which is which? There is, of course, an abundance of anecdotal evidence of garlic's effectiveness. You may even be personally acquainted with people who claim to benefit from garlic. But as we all know, this does not count as science.

Some of the conflicting study results probably stem from the different forms of garlic used in the studies. Did the study use fresh garlic, garlic powder, garlic tablets, garlic oil, freeze-dried garlic, or aged garlic extract? Some forms of garlic are obviously more effective than others, and some forms may be effective for one disorder but not for another.

Another possible explanation of the differences in study results is that human subjects have differences in their constitutions. If we look at it from the perspective of either traditional Chinese medicine or the Ayurvedic system, garlic is more effective for people of certain physiologies. In both traditions, as well as in Western herbology from the Renaissance era, garlic has very effective heating properties. In these traditions, garlic is quite helpful for individuals with a weak, cold, or deficient nature, but for someone who tends to be naturally ruddy skinned and hot natured (pitta in Ayurvedic medicine), too much garlic can overheat the system. Therefore, as you read about the health benefits of garlic, remember that there is almost always someone who will disagree.

Garlic has very effective heating properties and is helpful for people with a weak or cold nature.

Following is an overview of the information I have found about the health benefits of garlic for specific health conditions or areas of concern.

Garlic and Cholesterol

Although eating garlic provides us with many pleasures and benefits, the possibility that it can help prevent heart disease should be enough to make it loved by everyone. According to the National Institutes of Health, 61 million people in the United States have one or more types of cardiovascular disease. Heart disease is still the number-one killer in the United States, causing 958,775 deaths in 1999 and claiming one life every thirty-three seconds. This is especially sad when we think of how many of these deaths could have been spared with dietary and lifestyle changes. Coronary heart disease happens when fatty deposits and bloodclots block an artery leading to the heart. A stroke occurs when a vessel leading to the brain is clogged.

In 1948, about 5,000 residents of the small town of Framingham, Massachusetts, volunteered to be part of an ongoing medical study on heart disease. Thanks to these volunteers, the risk factors for heart disease became apparent. High levels of blood cholesterol, smoking, and physical inactivity were all discovered to be significant and avoidable risk factors. Other factors included high triglyceride levels, high homocysteine levels, high blood pressure, and diabetes. Also, the amount of clotting material in the blood and the time it takes for the blood to clot contributed to both heart attacks and strokes. Although today about 75 percent of the original Framingham participants have died, the study is being continued with their offspring.

A total cholesterol level that is less than 200 mg/dl is desirable. Your HDLs (remember "H" stands for "Heavenly") should be less than 40 mg/dl; LDLs ("L" stands for "Lowly") should be less than 100 mg/dl.

If you are at risk for heart disease, the best things you can do for yourself are to improve your eating habits, increase the amount you exercise, avoid smoking, and control your weight. If you still have high cholesterol, your doctor may prescribe a cholesterol-lowering drug. Of course, garlic is not a substitute for medical care, but all drugs have some undesirable side effects and if you alter your diet and exercise program before your cholesterol gets out of control and add garlic to your daily regime, it is possible that you can lower your cholesterol without drugs. According to several studies, garlic may lower total cholesterol and especially low-density lipoprotein (LDL), or "bad," cholesterol. In a 1998 paper titled "Excerpts From Recent Advances on the Nutritional Benefits Accompanying the Use of Garlic as a Supplement," sponsored by Pennsylvania State University and the National Cancer Institute, Dr. M. Steiner of East Carolina University spoke of the benefits of aged garlic extract in treating cardiovascular disease. He said that although the effects were somewhat mild, the fact that aged garlic extract reduced so many different risk factors for cardiovascular disease made it unique and potent. He also noted that no drug had such versatility.

Do all the experts agree on this? No; there is some conflicting research. One of the main explanations for this conflict is that although garlic is one of the most studied foods, there still is not enough data out there. Because garlic is so cheap, it has very little commercial value, especially when compared to prescription drugs. This makes it more difficult to get funding for garlic research than for pharmaceutical research. Although some studies have shown garlic to be ineffective, garlic proponents say that these studies either were done with inferior garlic supplements lacking the bioactive components of fresh garlic or were not conducted over a long enough time period. According to a paper written by Kathy J. Kemper, MD, MPH, there have been more than thirty-five human studies conducted since 1975 to evaluate garlic's ability to lower blood lipids. Dr. Kemper, associate professor of pediatrics at Harvard Medical School, prepared her paper, titled "Clinical Information Summary—Garlic (*Allium sativum*)," in conjunction with the Longwood Herbal Task Force and the Center for Holistic Pediatric Education and Research. In more than a dozen studies published between 1979 and 1993, there was an average improvement in serum cholesterol concentrations of 9 to 12 percent and a significant reduction in serum triglycerides in hyperlipidemic patients who were taking standardized garlic powder supplements of 600 to 900 milligrams daily. This improvement was noted within one month. Subsequent randomized trials, however, have had mixed results.

According to an article in the October 2000 issue of *Nutrition Action Newsletter,* garlic supplements were only effective in studies that lasted three months or less. According to a review article by the Agency for Healthcare Research and Quality (AHRQ) of the U.S. Department of Health and Human Services, "the evidence that garlic lowers cholesterol is inconclusive." However, the same article also says "that while garlic has little long-term effect on cholesterol, preliminary studies suggest that garlic might help prevent heart attacks by reducing blood clotting."

A study conducted by Benjamin Lau, MD, PhD, professor of microbiology, immunology, and surgery at Loma Linda University, showed that garlic became more, not less, effective at lowering cholesterol after several months of use. In Dr. Lau's three-part study using aged garlic extract, described in his book *Garlic and You* (Apple Publishing Company, 1999), the subjects' cholesterol levels not only did not improve during the first two months, but actually rose slightly. Dr. Lau believes that this may have happened because the garlic was moving the fats from the tissues to the blood. With continued garlic use, however, the excess serum lipids were broken down and excreted through the intestinal tract, thus, over time, lowering the cholesterol. Dr. Lau says the subjects were given four capsules of aged garlic extract a day.

Research has shown that garlic increases good cholesterol and decreases bad cholesterol.

In the final part of Dr. Lau's study, the team of researchers differentiated between low-density lipoprotein (LDL) cholesterol and high-density lipoprotein (HDL) cholesterol, and found that garlic increased the good HDL cholesterol and decreased the bad LDL cholesterol. In 65 percent of the subjects, they were able to observe a significant drop in both cholesterol and triglycerides. Dr. Lau believes that LDL cholesterol is most harmful when it has been oxidized, and that garlic's efficacy in preventing heart disease is due to its preventing the oxidation of LDL.

Curious about why 35 percent of the subjects did not respond to the garlic therapy, Dr. Lau's team reviewed the subjects' dietary histories and found that they were heavy meat eaters. These subjects regularly consumed steaks, pastries, and ice cream, particularly as part of their evening meal. When these subjects improved their diets while continuing the garlic supplements, their lipids were lowered. Dr. Lau concluded that garlic is most effective when combined with a healthful diet.

Garlic and Blood Pressure

High blood pressure, or hypertension, is called the "silent killer" because it does not produce overt symptoms in the initial, moderate stages. Chronic high blood pressure creates the risk of heart disease, stroke, and kidney disease. It is estimated that 40 percent of the adult U.S. population may have high blood pressure. Among people age sixty and over, one out of two has high blood pressure.

Blood pressure is represented by two numbers—the top (systolic) number signifies the pressure when the heart is beating. The bottom (diastolic) number represents the pressure when the heart is resting between beats. An optimal blood pressure reading is less than 120 / 80.

In the famous Dietary Approaches to Stop Hypertension (DASH) study, researchers found that a diet high in fruits, vegetables, and low-fat dairy products was almost as effective at lowering blood pressure as drugs. Other ways to help control blood pressure are maintaining optimal weight, avoiding caffeine and tobacco, consuming fewer than two alcoholic beverages per day for men and one for women, and not eating too much sugar. Exercise and stress reduction also help. Another contributing factor in hypertension is sodium intake. According to the American Dietetic Association, the average adult consumes eight to ten times more sodium than the body needs. The recommended sodium intake is 2,400 milligrams per day, including the sodium that occurs naturally in foods. To help you envision how much this is, one teaspoon of salt equals 2,000 milligrams.

Although there are many proponents of using garlic to lower blood pressure, including Dr. M. Steiner of East Carolina University, there is no conclusive scientific evidence to back the practice up. However, according to C. A. Silagy and H. A. Neil in their article, "A Meta-Analysis of the Effect of Garlic on Blood Pressure," published in the April 1994 issue of the *Journal of Hypertension,* "garlic may be of some clinical use in subjects with mild hypertension." The fact that garlic has not been proven to cure hypertension doesn't mean that it will not help, however. I personally know people—and you may know people, too—who swear that garlic assists them in controlling their blood pressure. One thing we can say for sure is that if you use garlic in cooking, your food will be so flavorful that your tendency to oversalt will be lessened.

Garlic and Detoxification

According to Dr. Lau in his book *Garlic and You,* garlic helps to detoxify heavy metals in the body. If this is true, it could be extremely valuable because in today's polluted environment, heavy-metal poisoning is more serious and more common than most people realize. Heavy metals such as lead, cadmium, cobalt, and mercury can be absorbed into our systems through exposure to substances such as polluted air, paints, drinking water, and contaminated fish. Mercury from dental amalgams is still controversial, but many people feel that it is a serious problem. Dr. Samuel Wong, a dentist from Honolulu who believes that amalgam fillings are detrimental, used garlic to reduce the levels of mercury in fourteen dental patients.

Garlic helps to detoxify heavy metals, which are quite damaging to the body.

Detoxifying the body is done through the liver, and Dr. Lau cites studies by Dr. Tohru Fuwa of the Central Research Laboratories of Wakunaga Pharmaceutical Company in Japan indicating that four of the sulfur compounds isolated from garlic protected liver cells from damage caused by the toxic chemical carbon tetrachloride. These findings were confirmed by Dr. Hiroshi Hikino and colleagues at the Pharmaceutical Institute of Tohoku University. Dr. Lau also claims that garlic nullifies the effects of radiation. A study from John Moores University in the United Kingdom found that aged garlic extract protected liver cells from exposure to the industrial solvent bromobenzene, which causes liver damage in vitro. These are just two of several studies that illustrate how garlic may become even more precious in the years to come if industrial pollution continues to worsen.

Garlic and Cancer

After heart disease, cancer is the most frequent cause of death in the United States. It may well be garlic's ability to detoxify that makes it useful in preventing cancer. Although there is no one "officially" agreed-upon cause of cancer, many researchers have concluded that exposure to chemical toxins may play a major role. An excellent and very readable book that supports this hypothesis is *Living Downstream* by biologist Sandra Steingraber (Addison-Wesley, 1997). Dr. Steingraber began researching the environmental causes of cancer after she was diagnosed, at a young age, with bladder cancer, a disease that had already affected several members of her *adopted* family.

In 2005, cancer became the leading cause of death in the United States.

In an article published in issue number 14 of the newsletter *The Cancer Chronicles,* Ralph W. Moss, PhD, writes that in a 1991 study, garlic was shown to stimulate the production of the enzyme glutathione S-transferase (GST). This enzyme occurs naturally in the body and protects against cancer by detoxifying potent carcinogens. According to a 1999 article on the website *BBC News,* a research team based in New Zealand concluded that one of garlic's compounds, DADS, produces enzymes in the gut that can clear the gut of cancer.

In one of Dr. Lau's many studies, he found that aged garlic extract and two other garlic compounds helped to prevent cancer caused by aflatoxin by attacking the aflatoxin in three different ways. Aflatoxin is the carcinogenic mold that contaminates peanuts, grains, beans, and sweet potatoes. First, garlic inhibits aflatoxin from binding to deoxyribonucleic acid (DNA). Second, it inhibits the metabolism of aflatoxin. And third, it increases the water-soluble metabolites in the body so that the carcinogenic compounds can be detoxified.

Eating garlic has been linked to lower rates of cancer.

There have also been several epidemiologic studies that linked garlic intake with lower rates of cancer across populations. In northern China, where people commonly eat five to ten cloves of garlic per day, there is a lower incidence of stomach cancer. Other studies have been done in Sweden, Italy, and the Netherlands that also showed lowered risk of stomach cancer in people who ate garlic. The Iowa Women's Health Study began in 1986 with 41,837 women who answered questions pertaining to their lifestyle habits. They were followed continuously in subsequent years. Four years after the start of the study, it was determined that the women who ate significant quantities of garlic were approximately 30-percent less likely to develop cancer of the colon. In one of the largest epidemiologic studies conducted, Dr. Lenore Arab and colleagues from the University of North Carolina at Chapel Hill analyzed seventeen international population studies examining the eating habits of more than 100,000 people. The highest consumers of garlic ate about six cloves per week. Based on six studies, the researches concluded that "high consumption of raw or cooked garlic decreases the risk of colorectal cancer from 10 percent to nearly 50 percent." Based on four studies, the people who ate the most garlic cut their risk of stomach cancer in half.

Garlic for Natural Pest Control

Garlic is an effective ingredient for natural pest control and can be found in numerous homemade as well as commercial formulas. Not only does garlic protect our health and make our food taste better, it helps protect our planet by giving us alternatives to dangerous poisons. A garlic-based insect repellent that you can buy is called Garlic Barrier Insect Repellent. It is a strong liquid garlic concentrate that dilutes in water and can be sprayed on farm and garden plants to keep insects off. It is registered with the Environmental Protection Agency (EPA), is completely nontoxic, and does not alter the taste or smell of the plant. If you cannot find this product in your local gardening center, see the Resource List beginning on page 181 for mail-order suppliers.

For do-it-yourselfers, the following is a recipe for a garlic-based pest control mixture that you can make at home. It is safe to use on plants.

GENERAL PEST SPRAY

This recipe will repel most insects, but it will not kill them. You can spray it on plants inside and outside your house. This mixture is most effective when used at dawn and dusk for three consecutive days.

1 cup grated castile soap or French olive oil soap

3 cups boiling water

1 cup tobacco

Cloves from 1 garlic bulb, peeled or unpeeled

1. Place the grated soap in a bowl and add one cup of the boiling water. Set aside.
2. Place the tobacco in a blender and pour in the remaining boiling water. Add the garlic and blend until smooth.
3. Strain the tobacco-garlic mixture through cheesecloth and discard the pulp. Pour into a spray bottle, add the dissolved soap, and shake to mix. Spray as needed for general pest control.

Doctors at the University of Texas Southwestern Medical Center in Dallas are a little more skeptical. They say that there is a possibility that the overall diets of the populations studied may have something to do with the results, suggesting that the people who ate the most garlic perhaps also ate the most vegetables. The doctors wisely suggest that although adding garlic to your diet could have health benefits, it is best not to rely on any one food to protect yourself from cancer. They recommend instead eating a varied diet rich in fruits and vegetables.

Garlic and Infection

Garlic has a long history of being used to inhibit certain viruses, fungi, bacteria, and parasites. Today, modern science is confirming what folk healers have long known—garlic can be successfully used to treat infections. One of the more interesting articles on this subject, published in 2001 on the website *BBC News*, was about a South African researcher at the Child's Health Institute in Cape Town, South Africa. This researcher, Dr. Sid Cywes, professor of pediatrics at the Red Cross Children's Hospital, discovered garlic's power against infections by chance. Dr. Cywes's favorite pastime is breeding and hybridizing a certain type of orchid that is native to South Africa. When the beakers storing his orchid cuttings became infected with a fungus, he consulted an old reference book and was led to attempt to control the problem with garlic. He was astonished by the results and decided to try garlic on human infections.

Both scientific research and traditional folk remedies have shown that garlic is a powerful antibiotic.

With the help of his colleague Dr. Peter de Vet, Dr. Cywes made a formula of two parts water to one part garlic and put it into a centrifuge to get rid of any lumps. The doctors then gave this solution to babies and children mixed with either milk or orange juice in a bottle. They found the solution to be especially valuable for treating children with infections who had been on antibiotics for a long time and had developed a resistance, or who had suffered side effects, such as oral thrush, from conventional antibiotics. Apparently, the children were not fond of the taste, but the mixture had no side effects. They have also used garlic in antibiotic creams for burns, and although it has not undergone a controlled clinical trial, the doctors are encouraged with the results. Drs. de Vet and Cywes also see promise for treating babies with human immunodeficiency virus (HIV) who have candida infections.

A group of high school teachers participating in the Woodrow Wilson Commuter Institute on Biodiversity, held in New York City at Pace University and the American Museum of Natural History in August 1999, conducted an interesting experiment. They created a project that tested the antimicrobial effects of different spices on bacterial growth. Their experiment was designed for a classroom setting as a multicultural activity, with the participants bringing in spices used in their homes to perform the experiment. Some of the spices they used were ginger, onion, curry, nutmeg, basil, jalapeño pepper, red pepper, black peppercorns, and, of course, garlic. The results of the experiment indicated that both ginger and garlic had antimicrobial effects on all the inocula, including *Escherichia coli* (*E. coli*) and *Bacillus cereus* (*B. cereus*), marsh mud, marsh water, and leaf litter. Mint demonstrated antimicrobial effects on *E. coli* and *B. cereus.* Thyme also had an effect on *B. cereus.* The antimicrobial action was demonstrated with fresh spices only. Dry, powdered spices had no effect.

Fresh and raw are usually thought to be the keys to the most potent antimicrobial effect of garlic because the active ingredient for this purpose is allicin, which, as we said earlier, is an unstable compound that is destroyed with heat and does not store well. However, there have been some experiments that have shown that freeze-dried garlic-juice powder is also effective against certain bacteria.

In a 1999 study at the Weizmann Institute of Science in Rehovot, Israel, it was found that allicin had a variety of antimicrobial activities. In its pure form, allicin was found to exhibit antibacterial activity against a wide range of bacteria, including multi-drug-resistant enterotoxicogenic strains of *E. coli.* It also was found to have antifungal activity, particularly against *Candida albicans,* and antiparasitic activity, against some major human intestinal protozoan parasites such as *Entamoeba histolytic* and *Giardia lamblia.* The same study found that garlic also had antiviral activity.

By now, you have seen how garlic's antimicrobial power is undisputed. But what does it do to beneficial bacteria? If garlic has the power to kill bacteria, does it also kill beneficial bacteria such as *Lactobacillus casei.* According to a paper from the American Society for Microbiology, a study conducted at Cardiff University in the United Kingdom has shown that it takes ten times more garlic to kill *Lactobacillus* than *E. coli.* Therefore, you do not have to worry about garlic killing off the healthy bacteria in your intestines. As you can see, garlic is forever acting both wisely and with consideration. Another amazing feature of garlic is that so far, there have been no reported cases of microorganisms developing resistance against it, which is not the case with conventional antibiotics.

Garlic and Candidiasis

Raw garlic and aged garlic extract are effective in controlling *Candida albicans,* especially when taken in conjunction with a healthy whole-foods diet that limits sugar and yeast.

Because candidiasis is such a widespread problem, I would like to emphasize garlic's effectiveness in treating it. *Candida albicans* is a yeastlike fungus that, according to researcher Hulda Clark, PhD, is everywhere, even flying through the air looking for a place to land. If it invades the mouth, the resulting condition is called thrush. It can affect the skin, the vagina, and the digestive track. Although we all have some candida in our intestines, when our immune systems are strong, we can keep it at bay. If it gets out of hand, candidasis results and can become a serious problem.

According to Paul Pitchford in *Healing With Whole Foods,* the symptoms of candida overgrowth include chronic tiredness, mental sluggishness, chronic vaginitis or prostatitis, anal itching, bloating and other digestive problems, bad breath, extreme sensitivity to tobacco smoke and chemical fumes, mucus in the stools, frequent colds, cravings for sweets and yeasted breads, recurrent fungal infections such as athlete's foot, and low immunity in general. Among the causes of candidiasis are repeated doses of broad-spectrum antibiotics and poor diet, especially eating too much sugar. Both raw garlic and aged garlic extract have been shown to be effective in controlling candida, especially in conjunction with a good whole-foods diet that includes probiotics ("friendly bacteria" supplements such as lactobacillus, streptococcus, and bifidus) and limits refined sugars, yeast, and fruit. If you think you have candida, see your healthcare practitioner to help you get started with treatment.

Garlic and Immunity

Most of the research that has been conducted on garlic and the immune system has been done with Kyolic Aged Garlic Extract and funded by the manufacturer. According to this research, aged garlic extract has been shown to be of help in controlling infectious diseases not only because of its antimicrobial activity, but also because it enhances the immune system. In a 1989 study by T. Abdullah and colleagues, it was found that aged garlic extract enhanced natural killer cell activity and improved helper-to-suppressor T cell ratios in patients with acquired immune deficiency syndrome (AIDS). In the study, it was found that aged garlic extract was more effective than high doses of raw garlic for enhancing natural killer cell activity.

In a 1999 study by E. Kyo and colleagues, aged garlic extract was shown to enhance the proliferation of spleen cells and to augment the immune-stimulating activity of various well-known immunostimulatory agents. In another study by Kyo and colleagues, it was found that garlic's antitumor activities were due in part to immune modulation. These are just three of several studies from Kyolic Research confirming the positive effects that aged garlic extract has on the immune system.

Garlic and Aging

Other health benefits attributed to garlic that have been studied include its antioxidant powers and its effect on aging. Antioxidants are substances that reduce the damage to the body caused by free radicals. Free radicals are formed when oxygen interacts with certain molecules during normal bodily processes or from exposure to pollutants. These free radicals damage cells and are hypotheti cally linked to aging and to the development of many illnesses. The antioxidants

Garlic reduces the damage to the body that is caused by free radicals.

include vitamins C and E, beta-carotene, and selenium. Garlic is a source of what is said to be a highly bioavailable form of selenium.

Perhaps the definitive illustration of garlic's health benefits, especially of its role in aging, is the example provided by the extraordinary Delaney sisters. Sadie and Bessie Delaney's lives were the subject of a play and a movie, as well as the wonderful, best-selling book *Having Our Say: The Delaney Sister's First 100 Years* (Kodansha International, 1993). The two sisters, whose father was a slave, lived amazingly active and accomplished lives. They lived together and remained vigorous, both physically and mentally, during their entire lives. Bessie died at 104 years old and Sadie died at 109. Their simple health regime included the avoidance of alcohol and tobacco. Every morning except Sunday, they practiced yoga and took a swallow of cod liver oil and a bite of guess what. You got it—garlic. They each ate a chopped clove of garlic. We may not all have the genetic potential of these two beautiful women, but we all can try to follow their example, especially with something as easy and pleasurable as eating garlic.

CONTRAINDICATIONS TO GARLIC USE

The most frequently mentioned side effect of garlic? Bad breath.

The most frequently mentioned side effect of garlic use is bad breath. Garlic, especially when eaten raw, can also cause indigestion in some sensitive individuals. In addition, prolonged contact with the skin can cause blistering.

Although garlic is not a drug, it is a strong substance that can react with certain drugs. Therefore, if you are taking any medications, you should consult with your physician before taking garlic supplements or eating large amounts of fresh garlic daily. Garlic may, for example, increase the potency of blood pressure medications. It is also believed to intensify the blood-thinning effects of aspirin and other drugs with blood-thinning properties, such as warfarin sodium (Coumadin). People with HIV who take saquinavir (Fortovase) should make sure to speak with their doctor before adding garlic to their diet or beginning garlic supplementation. Garlic supplements have been shown to decrease levels of this anti-HIV medication by 51 percent and are therefore likely to reduce its HIV-fighting activity. Garlic may also adversely affect diabetes medications because it may cause a decrease in blood sugar levels. Garlic is also contraindicated before surgery because of its potential anticlotting properties. For the same reason, pregnant women should discontinue garlic supplements two weeks prior to their due date.

Although none of the Western research that I have seen on garlic takes into consideration individual constitution types, Oriental medicine does. According to Paul Pitchford in *Healing With Whole Foods,* in traditional Chinese medicine, garlic is contraindicated in what are called heat conditions. A heat condition is when the patient has a red face and eyes, the sensation of feeling too hot, an aversion to heat, canker sores, and the desire for large quantities of cold drinks. Other symptoms for which garlic is contraindicated in traditional Chinese medicine are dry mouth; intermittent fever; fresh, red cheeks; night sweats; fast, thin pulse; and frequent but light thirst. These conditions are called heat symptoms related to yin deficiency. If you exhibit one or more of these symptoms, you may wish to consult with a doctor of Oriental medicine, an acupuncturist, or a practitioner of Ayurvedic medicine before introducing garlic supplements or large amounts of fresh garlic into your regime.

Folk remedies and the historic uses of garlic are perhaps not as wacky as they may seem at first glance. Modern science has given many of the powers purportedly held by our beloved garlic some serious credence, and although some of garlic's claims have not yet been proven without a doubt, neither can they be totally refuted. One thing that we do know for sure is that garlic is delicious, so indulge. It just might do you some good.

CHAPTER 5

Growing Garlic at Home

Each clove of garlic has a sacred power.

—HILDERIC FRIEND, MINISTER AND AUTHOR

Growing garlic, whether for pleasure, passion, or profit, is one of the nobler activities in which any human can engage. It allows us to enjoy and to share with others all of the wondrous gifts that our dear garlic has to give. The act of digging into the raw, fragrant earth, planting a seemingly insignificant little clove, nurturing it, and watching it become a tall and glorious plant is a humbling experience. It brings us into the rhythms of life and instills deep within our hearts a sense of connection with the Source of all being. Yes, garlic is not only a provider of nourishment, health, and culinary delights, it is a potential guru, a spiritual teacher with the power to strip away illusions of separateness while awakening us to the blissful perception of nature's wholeness.

It's true, gardeners and peasants possess a simple, ingrained wisdom that is spawned only by the type of patient, cyclical labor that is needed to make a garden grow. Gardening is a meditative process. It forces us to wait for nature to act in her own time. No one can impose his or her will upon Mother Nature. When people try, the results are disastrous. We must work with her, nurturingly and lovingly, allowing her to perform the miracle in which we play a minor yet essential role.

Growing garlic at home is a rewarding and enriching experience, and it does not require a move to either a farm or a monastery. In this chapter, I will tell you how to grow garlic in your own backyard, or even in containers on a patio or balcony. Health and sensual pleasures are gifts not to be negated, but the act of planting a clove, watching it grow, and reaping the rewards is the ultimate in garlic love—a realm reserved for the fortunate and adventurous few.

GARLIC GRASS IN A POT

You can easily grow garlic grass in a pot.

If you are intrigued by the prospect of growing garlic but are not yet ready to start digging up your backyard, you can grow garlic grass in a pot. You can do this outdoors on a patio or balcony, or even inside, year round, on a sunny windowsill. It is easy to do, and you can see results fast.

Start with any size flowerpot and fill it with a good quality, rich potting soil. Then take several unpeeled organic garlic cloves and plant them about one inch deep. Cloves that are too small to use in cooking are good for this. However, if you don't use either organic garlic or garlic seed stock, you may be disappointed because supermarket garlic is sometimes treated to keep it from sprouting. Plant as many cloves as will fit comfortably in the pot. Don't worry if they are a little crowded because garlic planted in this manner will not grow into bulbs. Water the garlic, and place the pot in a sunny location.

Keep the soil moist but not wet. Don't overwater or the cloves will rot. In about three weeks, your garlic sprouts should be about six inches tall and you can start snipping them with scissors to use as a delicious, garlicky garnish. The garlic grass will continue to flourish in the pot for about two to three months. Then you can start growing some new grass.

WHEN TO PLANT

Growing garlic is a bit like growing tulips or other bulbs. You plant them in the fall. They flower in the spring. Of course, with garlic you get a scape rather than a real flower. And then again, most softneck garlics don't even have a scape, so it is not really like growing tulips at all, except for the fact that tulip bulbs and garlic cloves are both planted at around the same time.

Although I can't give you an exact planting time, in most parts of the United States, garlic is planted from mid September to early October, or until four to six weeks before the ground freezes. The ideal soil temperature for planting it is around 60 degrees Fahrenheit. In the North (planting zones 3 through 6), spring planting is possible, but the bulbs will be smaller and the harvest will be later. In the South (planting zones 7 through 10), garlic can be planted from September to as late as January or March. But if the ground does not freeze for at least two weeks, the garlic must be cold-treated by refrigeration at 40 degrees Fahrenheit for forty days. The technical name for this is "vernalization."

If you are still not certain when to plant garlic in your area, you can always call or visit your local agricultural extension service. This service is one of the best things about the United States. It exists practically everywhere, and its sole purpose is to provide you with helpful advice regarding anything you might wish to know about gardening. It's free, and the people who work there really love to help. They are so nice that you may feel like you are imposing on them, but it's their job and they are paid to do it. So, take advantage of this great service. It can save the novice gardener from making lots of mistakes.

If you are a novice, it is also a good idea to seek out other gardeners in your area who grow garlic. Gardeners are an especially friendly lot. I have never met one that I didn't like. They love to talk about gardening and share their secrets with anyone who is interested enough to listen. In my humble-yet-opinionated view, the world would be a much better place if more people gardened, and every gardener I know feels exactly the same way, which is why they are eager to teach.

Hardneck garlic grows better in the northern parts of the U.S., while softnecks thrive in the southern parts.

WHAT TYPE OF GARLIC TO PLANT

After you have determined when to plant your garlic, you must decide what kind of garlic to plant. If you are a novice, it is better to select a variety that is acclimated to your growing conditions. As a rule of thumb, hardnecks do better in the North and softnecks do better in the South. Furthermore, softnecks grow better in the North than hardnecks do in the South. Because there is such a large variety of garlics and so many different soil and growing conditions around the country, a good way to decide which type of garlic to grow in your area might be to talk to either a local grower or your local extension service. If there is a farmer's market near you where local farmers sell their produce, this is perhaps your best place to gather both information and seed stock. If someone is already successfully growing a certain garlic variety in your area, you know it will work.

You can also reread Chapter 3, "Garlics of the World," to help you decide which garlic varieties appeal to you and which ones grow well in your general area. If the garlic you wish to try is not available locally, check the Resource List on page 181 for mail-order suppliers. Most of the merchants that sell specialty garlics will be happy to help you select your first seed stock.

Garlic from the supermarket may or may not grow. As we said in Chapter 2, most of the garlic in the supermarket is one of two types—California Early or California Late. These garlics prefer a temperate, Mediterranean-type climate, so if you live in the South, they may be the garlic for you. But beware. Much of the commercial garlic that is available in supermarkets has been treated with either irradiation or a sprout inhibitor to keep it from sprouting, so for planting purposes it is worthless.

PREPARING THE SOIL

Growing garlic is easy, but don't be in a hurry. Start in the summer to get your soil ready for fall planting, and you will be glad you did. Whether you are planting a field for commercial purposes or a backyard patch or container garden for personal pleasure, the most important factor in achieving a successful crop is rich, healthy soil. Good soil grows healthy plants. This bit of common sense is something that gardeners and farmers have known since the beginning of agriculture. It was forgotten only in the twentieth century, when people thought they could outsmart nature with chemicals and poisons. If your soil is rich, your crop will taste better, need less water, and be more resistant to diseases and insects.

Tilling the soil will help grow healthier plants.

Garlic loves rich, loamy soil, so it is worth the effort to enrich it by adding compost or manure. The experts say that the perfect pH (acid-alkaline balance) for garlic is 6.5, but I have gardened for years without ever knowing the pH of my soil. I just add manure and compost, then mulch it over. Soil is alive with microorganisms and insects that contribute to its—and our—health. In today's conventional farming, the plant—not the soil—is fed. This creates inferior plants that need expensive and dangerous poisons to protect them from insects and diseases. This in turn kills the beneficial insects, poisons the soil, and leeches into our water supply. It is dangerous to humans, pets, and wild animals. According to an EPA estimate, in 1997, home and garden consumption accounted for 76 million pounds of pesticide active ingredients. The active ingredients in pesticides are the ones designed to kill or damage a pest. Most pesticides also have inert ingredients, which are added to make the pesticide more potent, easier to spray or sprinkle, or such. The inert ingredients, however, are not necessarily harmless. About one fourth of inert ingredients have been classified as hazardous by a state, federal, or international agency. Furthermore, pesticide manufacturers are not required to identify all the inert ingredients in their products. In addition, they are required to perform only minimal testing. So, if you decide to grow garlic, please, for the sake of the planet, do not add to these obscene statistics. Contrary to what the poison peddlers might tell you, garlic, and anything else for that matter, grows just fine without it.

If your backyard is like those of most Americans, it is probably covered with grass. Therefore, you will have to get rid of the grass in the spot where you would like to grow your garlic. One of the easiest, least toxic ways to kill grass will also kill any weeds and pathogens in the soil. It is a simple method, called solarization, that involves covering your planting area with plastic and allowing the sun's heat to kill the weeds. (For specific directions, see page 107.) Interestingly, solarization does not harm the helpful microorganisms in the soil. In fact, it seems to benefit them. The best time to solarize is when the sun is at its hottest, at mid summer. This is perfect timing for garlic because you will not be planting until the fall anyway.

In areas that get lots of rain, it is best to plant garlic in raised beds, which allow the soil to drain.

It is not necessary to make raised beds, but it is helpful if you live in an area that gets a lot of rain. Raised beds help the soil to drain so that the garlic does not become infected with fungi. Therefore, when you start to think about your plot size, you may also want to consider making a border that extends about three feet farther than the planting area. This way, you can take some soil from the border and pile it onto the planting area to make the planting area higher than the surrounding land. Mulch the border to keep it weed-free and to create an area where you can stand or kneel when you tend your crop.

An easier way to make a raised bed, but one that involves a small expense, is to buy some top soil and pile it onto your planting area along with the compost or manure. Add enough to raise the area about one foot. Sometimes boards or railroad ties are suggested to box in a raised bed, but they are not necessary. In addition, if the wood is pressure-treated or creosote-treated, harmful toxins could leach into the soil.

PLANTING THE CLOVES

To plant your garlic crop, carefully separate the outer cloves from the garlic bulbs you purchased for planting; try not to tear the clove wrappers. Choose only the

Solarizing Your Growing Area

One of the tasks that prevents many a wannabe gardener from actually getting out the gardening gloves is the daunting chore of clearing a spot for the crop. Getting down on your knees and pulling out the grass and weeds by hand can be time consuming and tiring. A better method is solarization, which utilizes the sun's rays to kill the grass, weeds, and any pathogens in that perfect spot for your garlic. The only requirement is that the planting bed be at least three-feet wide by three-feet deep. (If the grass, weeds, and pathogens are not killed as well around the edges of the plot, where it may not get as hot under the plastic, you will still have enough room left to plant at least some garlic.)

The following five easy steps will help you solarize your chosen plot of land and get your garlic crop off to a good start.

1. Gather your supplies. These include compost or manure, a small rotary tiller, a shovel, a rake, a sprinkler or soaker hose, and enough 3- or 6-millimeter clear plastic sheeting to cover your plot in a single layer and overlap each side by at least a foot. Note that you can rent a rotary tiller from your local tool rental shop.

2. Spread a generous layer of the compost or manure over the area you wish to plant, then till it under with the small rotary tiller until it has a consistent texture with no large dirt clods. If you have rocky soil, remove the rocks.

3. Dig a trench about eight inches deep all around the plot, piling the extra soil over the planting area. Rake over the entire plot until the surface is even and smooth.

4. Using the sprinkler or soaker hose, water the entire bed evenly until the water has seeped down at least a foot into the soil.

5. Cover the plot with the plastic sheeting, overlapping it by at least a foot on all sides. Stretch the plastic as tight as you can, then weigh down the edges with rocks or bricks over the trench.

The above five steps are the easy part. The hard part is waiting for the sun to do its job. In cooler climates, such as New England and the Midwest, this should take about eight to ten weeks. In warmer climates, such as the South, four to six weeks should suffice, but you may wish to leave the plastic in place for eight weeks to be sure the solarization is complete. To prevent new weeds from sprouting in your bed, you can leave the plastic on until you are ready to plant.

largest and most perfect cloves for planting. Do this on the day you plant or the day before because if you do it too far in advance, the cloves will lose some of their vigor. Reserve the small cloves for eating or for making garlic grass in a pot, and discard any damaged cloves.

Plant the cloves with the flat end down and pointed side up. In mild climates, plant them about two inches deep; in colder climates, plant them two to four inches deep. Space the cloves about six inches apart, in rows that are about fifteen to eighteen inches apart. Mulch your babies with about a six-inch covering of leaves or clean straw, and forget about them until springtime.

TENDING THE CROP

In late winter to early spring, you will begin to see beautiful young garlic shoots pushing their way up through the mulch. At this time, if you desire, you can apply an organic fertilizer or some liquid fish emulsion or liquid seaweed; follow the directions on the package. If you added a lot of compost or manure before you planted, you may not need to fertilize.

Be sure to keep your garlic bed weeded because garlic does not compete well with weeds. Using a hoe, you can cultivate around the plants if the ground becomes hard. Just be sure to keep the hoe far enough away from the garlic to avoid damaging it.

Garlic likes moist but not wet soil, and the best way to know if you need to water is to stick your hand a few inches down into the soil to see if it feels damp. If it is dry, you should water. Overwatering garlic can result in the growth of fungus, which will ruin your crop.

If you planted hardneck garlic, it will send up a scape, or seed stalk, sometime in the early part of the summer. These scapes are delicious, so cut them while they are still tender and eat them. There is a lot of controversy among garlic gardeners about exactly when to cut the scape, which makes me believe that the timing is not all that important. Most varieties of softneck garlic usually do not send up a scape, but sometimes, in times of stress, they will.

Braiding Garlic

Garlic braids add a decorative yet functional accent to any kitchen, and they also make great gifts. You may wish to try your hand at braiding garlic if you have some softnecks in your garden. The following instructions from Donna Metcalfe make it easy. Donna has a very special online aromatherapy store with a metaphysical twist called Good Scents (www.goodscents.org).

Garlic can be braided when it is fresh out of the garden. Just choose some well-formed, large heads and rinse them off before you start, since garlic for braiding should be clean and pretty. It is possible to braid garlic after it has dried for a few days, but don't wait too long or the leaves will become brittle. Braiding garlic is like braiding hair, except that you start from the bottom and go up rather than starting at the top and braiding down.

To braid garlic, take three heads and arrange them as shown in Figure A. Braid the leaves together once or twice, close to the garlic heads. Braid them tightly so that the leaves don't show in between. Add a fourth head of garlic above the center one; include its leaves with any one of the others and braid a little more, as shown in Figure B. Next, add two more heads, this time to the sides. Include their leaves with the others and keep braiding, as shown in Figure C. Add one, then two, and then one garlic head again, until the braid is as long as you want—or until you run out of garlic.

For the best-looking braids, keep the heads close together. When Donna braids for herself, however, she is more concerned with ease of use than appearance, so she braids loosely to make it easier to break off the garlic heads as she needs them.

To finish, braid the remaining leaves together, tie them with twine, and trim the ends. Hang the braid up to allow the garlic to dry.

A

B

C

HARVESTING AND CURING THE BULBS

If you read Chapter 3, "Garlics of the World," you know that the different garlics mature at different times. But no matter what specific type of garlic you are growing, at some point in mid summer, the beautiful green leaves of your garlic plants will begin to die. This will mean that harvest time is near, so keep a close watch during the next couple of weeks. When there are only about five green leaves left on the plants, it will be time to harvest. Don't wait too long because the bulbs will break apart.

To harvest your bulbs, carefully dig under them with a garden fork to loosen the dirt around them. With a year in the making, your garlic bulbs are precious, so be careful not to cut into them when you dig them out. Bruised or damaged bulbs cannot be stored. After you have loosened the soil, pull the plants out and brush off the dirt. It is best not to wash them, but if you feel the need, do it quickly with a strong spray of water and make sure to let them dry immediately. Again, take care not to harm them.

To cure your bulbs, tie six to eight plants together in bundles and hang them in a cool, dry, airy shed or garage. The curing should take about ten to fourteen days, depending on the weather conditions. When the outer skins of the bulbs are dry and parchmentlike, you can take the garlic down. Cut off the leaves and trim the roots to about a half inch.

To store your garlic, place it in mesh bags. Keep it in a cool, dry, well-ventilated spot that preferably is dark. Do not store it in a home refrigerator because the high humidity will cause it to sprout or mold. Under proper conditions, garlic keeps for three to five months.

For the serious gardener as well as the neophyte, the act of planting an insignificant clove of garlic and watching it grow into a tall, magnificent plant is deliciously gratifying. Whether your crop is a pretty little pot of garlic grass on your windowsill or a glorious emerald field, if you put forth the effort you can harvest the rewards so graciously offered by our dear friend garlic. Don't you wish that your human lovers would be so kind?

PART TWO

The **Tastes** & **Pleasures** of **Garlic**

CHAPTER 6

Garlic Tips, Tricks, and Tools

How anything as small and delicate looking as a clove of garlic can have such an impact on food never ceases to amaze.

—BETSY BALSLEY, FOOD EDITOR, *LOS ANGELES TIMES*

It's time for the fun to begin! You have learned about garlic's history, health benefits, and cultivation. You have learned about the garlic products you can buy and the special varieties you can try. Now, let's get to the point and start putting this knowledge to use in the kitchen, where it belongs.

It's one thing to love garlic, but for that love to be truly fulfilled, you must go to the kitchen, roll up your sleeves, and dive in. If you don't actually cook with garlic, you cannot call yourself a true *amant.* To master the fine art of garlic cuisine, however, you do not have to spend hours slaving over a hot stove. Great cooking can and should be easy and not too time consuming. The recipes in this book were designed to be used, enjoyed, and personalized. The main thing to remember is that a better-than-average meal always starts with better-than-average ingredients. In my opinion, the most precious cooking skill that anyone can acquire is the knack of choosing high-quality ingredients. It may take a weekly drive out to a local organic farm, or even a little home gardening, but fresh, seasonal ingredients yield far greater results than any fancily wrapped gourmet store product or commercial-quality appliance when it comes to food preparation. Americans always talk about the fabulous food in Europe. Why is it so good? It is good because it emphasizes fresh regional ingredients prepared in their season. The tomatoes you buy out of season at the supermarket cannot compare with the ones you pick from your garden in season, and neither can the sauces made from each. So, if you want your cooking to be as fabulous as the garlic that you put into it, start with quality ingredients. It's as simple as that.

There are, however, a few tricks of the trade—techniques to make your garlic-cooking experience easier and more satisfying. So, in this chapter, we will look at garlic cookery, gadgets, tips, and techniques that will help you to indulge in your passion with ease and pleasure.

GARLIC TOOLS AND GADGETS

A good painter always buys the best brushes, but it's the artist, not the tool, that makes the painting. The tool is only a tool, and a great artist can create a masterpiece with a child's crayon set. The same is true in the kitchen. Many are the times that I have been in an extraordinary restaurant in France where scrumptious and beautifully presented meals were churned out with lighting speed from a kitchen smaller than many of us have in our homes. Nonetheless, good tools can be of service, and garlic has probably inspired more tools and gadgets than any other vegetable—or is that "herb"? Most garlic gadgets are inexpensive, and most of them are small, but they do take up kitchen space, and if your kitchen is like mine, space is precious. The more clutter in the kitchen, the less efficient the cook. So, you may want to consider which tools are best for you before buying everything that is out there. Following are the ones I have found useful.

Garlic Press

The one garlic tool that I would have a hard time living without is a garlic press. A garlic press, of course, presses garlic cloves into a juicy, pulpy purée. Pressed garlic imparts much more flavor to food than chopped or minced garlic, but more about this later.

If you buy a garlic press, make sure that it is a good one because there are some on the market that are not worth a dime. They do not work, they require the strength of Hercules, or they break after the kind of vigorous use any true garlic lover gives them. About twelve years ago, after going through three or four cheap garlic presses in a year's time, I decided to try to find a good one in France. What I found was a Swiss-made Zyliss Suzi Delux garlic press, and it is still with me today after having gotten an almost daily workout all these years. It is the only garlic press I own. Back when I purchased mine, they were not readily available in the United States. But today, they are easy to come by. The Zyliss Suzi Delux is so strong and well made that you can even press whole cloves without peeling them. It comes with a little plunger for easier cleaning and costs only about $14. It is a great buy, even if you are not an ardent garlic lover but just flirt with the bulb on occasion. I also hear that the Tupperware press is good, but I haven't tried it.

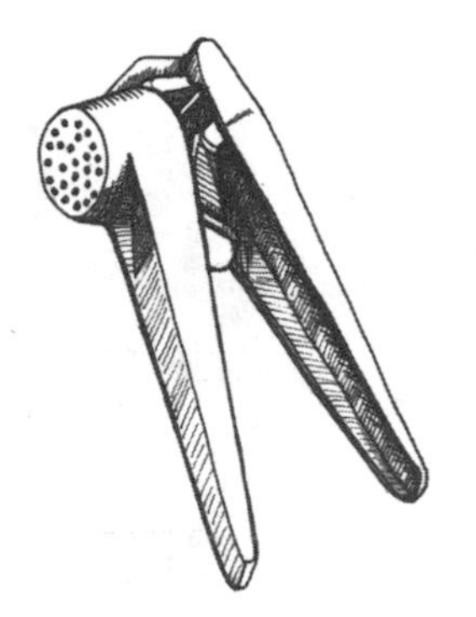

Garlic Press

Pressed garlic provides much more flavor than chopped or minced, so a garlic press is an essential tool for any garlic lover.

If you process large quantities of garlic, you may wish to have a garlic slicer and shredder. With this gadget, a plunger quickly pushes the garlic through a chute into a blade, which slices it quickly and easily. It is a small, plastic-and-stainless-steel contraption that flips over to shred and comes apart to clean. Another high-volume press that does several cloves at a time is called the Grate-CHEF Press. It works by screwing down over the cloves like a wine or olive press, and it will also grate cheese. The GrateCHEF Press is about three inches square and five inches high. Both the garlic slicer and shredder and the Grate-CHEF Press cost around $10. If you use large quantities of pressed garlic, you may find the GrateCHEF Press useful. Personally, when I press garlic, it is because I will be using it raw and therefore do not need such huge quantities. If you use a food processor to chop or slice vegetables, you may enjoy the garlic slicer and shredder. However, I prefer a sharp knife and cutting board, which are easier to clean than any gadget and, with a little practice, are just as fast, when taking the cleanup time into account.

Garlic Peeler-Roller

Another cool tool is the garlic peeler-roller. In some ways, this is the perfect gadget—cheap, small, easy to store, no moveable or breakable parts, and it works. It consists of simply a little rubber tube into which you insert your cloves of garlic. You roll this ingenious little gem on the countertop while exerting a light pressure with the palm of your hand and voilà! The skin falls right off.

They say that a harried husband invented the garlic peeler-roller because his wife always gave him the tedious job of peeling the garlic cloves when she cooked. I have seen these rollers priced anywhere from $6.99 to $8.95. That doesn't seem like much for what it does, but when you think about what it is, it looks like someone may be making a good profit. Well, I guess genius should be rewarded. But you can also buy a little rubber mat that will do the same thing for $2.50. When I discovered this, I looked through my drawer of unused kitchen gadgets and found a little rubber square intended to help unscrew hard-to-open lids and caps. It is about three inches by four inches in size and peels garlic beautifully. I just wrap it around the clove and roll it on the counter while pressing down lightly. You probably have plenty of items around your house that you could effectively use to peel garlic, such as a piece of material cut off the edge of an old rubber yoga mat.

Garlic Peeler-Roller

This inexpensive gadget makes easy work out of the tedious job of peeling garlic cloves.

Anyhow, if you don't want to wrack your brain trying to find the perfect material with which to construct a garlic peeler, you may just want to spring for the $2.50 plus shipping or even get the fancy tube model for a few dollars more. Any way you cut it, these little rubber things do peel garlic, and peeling garlic can get quite tedious when you use a lot of it. I have seen more expensive mechanical garlic peelers advertised, but I have not tried them. Frankly, when something this cheap works so well, why bother trying something pricier?

Garlic Roaster

Garlic roasters are decorative unglazed terracotta vessels with lids that are used for baking garlic. They are not essential, but they are cute and can be placed on the table, over a trivet, to serve roasted garlic bulbs to your guests. If you eat a lot of roasted garlic, you may want to have one.

The prices of garlic roasters vary depending on the roaster's size and whether it was mass produced or made by an artisan. A simple, small, one-bulb roaster costs under $10, while a larger one that will hold up to six cloves costs under $20. The larger garlic roaster can also be used for heating and serving small tortillas. Some garlic roasters suggest that you soak the lid before baking.

If you do not wish to purchase a garlic roaster, you can use a little piece of aluminum foil. Aluminum foil works just fine, and in fact, it may take you about ten minutes less to roast your garlic.

Garlic Roaster

Decorative terracotta roasters are used for both baking and serving garlic.

Garlic Keeper

Garlic keepers also are mostly for decoration. And again, like garlic roasters, their prices vary greatly depending on how and where they were made. You can find a simple garlic keeper for under $10, or you can pay over $50 for a beautiful, hand-painted one.

The main thing to remember when choosing a garlic keeper is that garlic has to breathe, so if the keeper has a lid, it must have air holes in the pot or the garlic will mold. Some garlic keepers are glazed outside but unglazed inside. An unglazed interior allows the absorption of moisture, keeping the garlic mold-free. I keep my garlic in a little antique brass pot that hangs from the wall in my kitchen. It was not made to hold garlic, but it does the job well, holding about six bulbs at a time. It is also quite pretty, and since it does not have a lid, it allows the air to circulate around the garlic.

If you'd like to purchase garlic peelers, peeler-roasters, roasters, or keepers, see the information in the Resource List on page 181.

GARLIC COOKING TECHNIQUES

Press some raw garlic into your recipe for robust, fiery flavor; cook your garlic whole for a milder, sweeter taste.

Like any great lover, garlic can be either hot and spicy, or gentle and tender. It all depends on how you treat it. This dual aspect of garlic's personality allows for incredible culinary diversity, permitting you to indulge in the bulb whether you desire a bold and brazen blast of heat or a sweet and subtle caress.

The secret to mastering the many facets of garlic's extraordinary nature is very simple, but it is based upon garlic's extremely complex chemical makeup. In Chapter 4, "Garlic and Your Health," we discussed how garlic does not have an odor when the cloves are whole and undamaged. This is because garlic's characteristic odor and flavor come from allicin, which is created from a chemical reaction that happens when the clove is cut or crushed. The more the clove is crushed, the more allicin is released and the stronger the clove will taste. Therefore, if you want to take a walk on the wild side of garlic gastronomy, all you need to do is press the clove and add it to your dish raw. Pressing brings out every bit of fire and flavor that a clove can muster. This is why recipes that call for raw garlic pressed in at the end of cooking use relatively little garlic.

To tame garlic, you need a little patience. Remember that allicin is volatile, and like passion, it doesn't stay around forever. Cooking transforms it into gentler compounds, and so, like love, does aging it. With this in mind, you can see how you can tame your fiery flame by cooking it nice and slowly. Even raw garlic can be subdued by letting it macerate in oil for a few hours.

If you really want your garlic to be mild mannered and well behaved, keep it whole when you cook it. When cloves of garlic are cooked whole, they do not develop allicin at all. In fact, it is possible to eat an entire bulb of garlic roasted, or even simmered in a soup or stew, without feeling overwhelmed.

Now, let's briefly reiterate what we just discussed. To get the most kick out of the least amount, press the garlic into a recipe without cooking it. However, if you wish to tame the beast, keep it whole and cook it slowly. The longer you cook garlic, the milder and sweeter it will be. For the ultimate garlic kick, press one or more cloves into a soup, bean dish, salad dressing, or stew just before serving. You can also achieve different degrees of garlic strength by cutting it into different-size pieces and cooking it for different lengths of time. However, don't think that you can achieve a mellow flavor in dishes by adding large pieces or whole raw cloves, because chewing raw garlic releases the allicin the same way that pressing it does. The only difference is that it is released in your mouth instead of in the recipe.

Another way to enjoy garlic's multifaceted personality is to get to know some of the different types of garlics that we discussed in Chapter 3, "Garlics of the World." There are garlics that are naturally mild, such as the Simoneti and the Persian Star, and there are others that are naturally strong, such as the Wild Buff. There are even garlics with a more moderate kick, somewhere in between the two extremes, such as the Music. The real connoisseur will get to know several varieties of garlic and use them according to the effects called for in particular dishes.

Now that you know some of the secrets of successfully using garlic in your recipes, let's examine the best ways to peel it. The ease with which you can peel your garlic can make the difference between enjoying the process of garlic cookery and considering it a chore.

PEELING GARLIC

If you can plan in advance and are not in a hurry, an easy way to peel garlic without a gadget is to soak it in water. That's right, just separate the cloves from the bulb and drop them into a little bowl of water. Let them soak for about an hour; the specific amount of time needed depends on the type of garlic. Sometimes thirty minutes is all it takes to loosen the skins, and other times it can take up to two hours. I have read that cold water works best, but I don't see any difference between cold and room-temperature water. Anyhow, after the cloves have soaked, you can peel off the skins almost like you peel a banana.

Smashing a garlic clove with the flat side of a knife is one way to loosen the skin.

Then there is the old trick of smashing the cloves with the edge of a knife. Place the garlic clove on a cutting board, place a knife with a wide blade over the clove, and whack the knife with the heel of your hand to slightly crush the clove. This causes the skin to loosen. If you don't have a knife with a wide blade, you can use the flat bottom of a glass. The only disadvantage of this method is that you cannot keep the clove whole and undamaged.

You can also use one of the garlic peelers that we just discussed. The little tubular rubber ones are great, and so are the rubber mat ones. Another ploy of the gourmet garlic cook is to use easy-to-peel varieties of garlic, such as any one of the rocamboles or porcelains. The trouble with the easy-to-peel garlics, however, is that they don't last as long as the other garlic varieties. Therefore, even though they are a joy to use in their season, they will not get you through the year. Because of this, most garlic lovers use a combination of easy-to-peel garlics and peeling techniques.

GARLIC ODOR ON THE HANDS

To get rid of garlic odor on your hands, just rub your hands over the back of a stainless steel spoon while holding them under running water. Finish by washing your hands with soap. I did not believe this one until I tried it, and then I was amazed. About three minutes later, however, a faint garlic odor returned. Rubbing your hands with lemon juice and salt also works pretty well but not perfectly. If you are really adamant about banishing garlic odor from your hands, try both these methods together. Together they appear to be more effective than either one alone.

GARLIC BREATH

If you are expecting me to give you a solution to garlic breath, don't hold your breath. Although many people offer cures for garlic breath, I have to say that they don't really work. If you know a truly effective one, please let me know. However, when you think about it, garlic breath is a small price to pay for the benefits and pleasures you can derive from eating the stinking rose.

Although I eat lots of garlic, rarely do people complain that I have garlic breath. There are three possible explanations for this: One, I don't have garlic breath. Two, my friends are exceptionally polite. Three, my friends also have garlic breath. Of these three explanations, I believe that number three is the most realistic. As more and more people are becoming lovers of garlic, more have garlic breath and don't notice it on other people. I also believe that good digestion helps to diminish the intensity of garlic breath. This has probably not been scientifically proven, but I have a feeling that it may be true.

When discussing cures for garlic breath, I am sure that you have heard the one about chewing fresh parsley or mint. I guess that this may help a little bit, and I'm sure that it is more effective than simply brushing your teeth or using mouthwash, which do not work. Some people say that chewing fennel seeds will help. This last one makes the most sense to me because fennel is an herb that helps digestion, and if my digestion theory is correct, fennel would help. Others say that the combination of parsley and sunflower seeds eaten after the garlicky meal is the best way to reduce garlic breath. It sounds better to me than chewing whole coffee beans, which is also sometimes recommended.

Purported "cures" for garlic breath include chewing fresh parsley, mint, fennel seeds, or coffee beans!

In the end, though, perhaps the test of a true garlic lover is how willing he or she is to reek—because the only way to enjoy the health benefits of garlic without the scent is to use odorless products, and that takes away all the fun. So, if you are brave enough to go out into the world with garlic on your breath, let's continue with some final tips for using garlic that will set you well on your way to garlic epicurism.

PRESERVING GARLIC

A time comes in most garlic lovers' lives when they suddenly go overboard. Gardening types will become so enamored with the stinking rose that they plant and harvest more than they can possibly eat. Others, drawn into a passion-induced frenzy, go to their local farmers market and buy cases of precious and perishable garlic with no idea of how they can possibly consume it all before it spoils. Both scenarios necessitate the exploration of methods of garlic preservation. As we all know, garlic preserved by any method is not a substitute for fresh, but it does have its own charms and advantages, especially when fresh garlic is out of season. Different methods of preserving garlic lend themselves to their own culinary uses, so explore them all and see which ones best suit your needs.

Before we examine the specific preservation methods, I want to emphasize that preserving garlic in oil is not safe unless the garlic oil is frozen. Garlic is a low-acid food and oil provides an oxygen-free environment, a combination that allows the growth of the bacteria *Clostridium botulinum,* which causes botulism. However, if you follow the methods in this book for freezing garlic-and-oil mixtures and keep them frozen until needed, it is safe.

Since we are discussing the potential dangers of preserving garlic, I would like to bring up a peculiar aspect of garlic's personality that is a bit disconcerting but not dangerous. Garlic sometimes changes color. It turns blue when its sulfur compounds come into contact with copper. Not much copper is needed for this to happen. The water in some areas of the United States contains enough copper to cause this reaction. Copper utensils can also instigate a color change in garlic. If garlic is harvested before maturity or is not allowed to completely dry, it can turn green in the presence of acid, such as from lemon. These color changes, as bizarre as they are, do not harm the garlic. It is still safe to eat.

Although garlic may change color to blue or green, it is still safe to eat.

There are six excellent methods for preserving garlic. They are freezing garlic, drying garlic, garlic vinegar, garlic salt, garlic oil, and refrigerator garlic pickles.

Freezing Garlic

Perhaps the easiest way to preserve garlic is to freeze it. Just peel the cloves and place them in freezer bags in the freezer. Easier yet, simply place the unpeeled garlic in freezer bags and remove cloves as needed. With both these methods, the cloves become a little mushy when they are thawed, but their flavor remains good.

Another method for freezing garlic is to chop it and wrap it tightly in plastic wrap. With this method, you can simply grate or break off small amounts of chopped garlic as needed, which is helpful for cooks who often must quickly throw a meal together.

You can also freeze garlic that has been pureéd in oil. This is nice because the oil keeps the mixture from freezing solid and it can be spooned out as needed, another help for busy cooks. To make frozen garlic oil pureé, place one part peeled garlic cloves in a blender or food processor along with two parts olive oil. Pureé the mixture, then immediately transfer it to a freezer container. Cover the container and place it in the freezer. Do not store garlic oil pureé at room temperature or in the refrigerator because the mixture can support the growth of *Clostridum botulinum* bacteria.

Drying Garlic

Peel the garlic, making sure to discard any bruised or damaged cloves. Cut the cloves in half lengthwise, place them in an electric food dehydrator, and follow the manufacturer's instructions for drying.

If you do not have a food dehydrator, you can dry the garlic in your oven. Make drying racks by stretching cheesecloth over the oven racks and securing it with toothpicks. Place the garlic on the racks and turn the oven to 140 degrees Fahrenheit for two hours, then lower it to 130 degrees until the garlic is completely dry and crisp.

Store garlic vinegar in the refrigerator, where it will keep for about four months.

Garlic Vinegar

To make garlic vinegar, take a bottle of white or red wine vinegar and drop in either whole or chopped garlic. Use as much garlic as you wish, as long as it is completely submerged in the vinegar. Store your garlic vinegar in the refrigerator and use both the vinegar and the garlic in salad dressings or any dish that calls for both vinegar and garlic. Garlic vinegar will keep, refrigerated, for about four months. If mold develops, discard the mixture.

Garlic Salt

Place dried garlic in a blender and process it until it turns to powder. Add four parts sea salt for each one part garlic powder and process for just a second or two to combine the two ingredients. Do not process the garlic salt too long because it will cake. Store the garlic salt in an airtight glass jar.

Garlic Oil

Fresh garlic and oil are a dangerous combination if left at room temperature. Because of garlic's low acidity and oil's lack of oxygen, they can cause botulism toxin to develop. However, peeled cloves of garlic can be added to oil and stored in the freezer for several months.

Commercially prepared garlic in oil contains a preservative to increase the acidity of the mixture and keep it safe. To make garlic-flavored oil at home, add dehydrated garlic to olive oil in a wide-mouth jar, screw on the lid, and place the jar in the refrigerator. If the olive oil turns solid, just spoon it out. Be careful, however, to always use a dry spoon.

As long as garlic stays submerged in vinegar, it will keep indefinitely in the refrigerator.

Refrigerator Garlic Pickles

Loosely fill a glass jar with peeled garlic cloves. Add enough red or white wine vinegar to cover the garlic and then add about one tablespoon of sea salt per cup of vinegar. Dried (not fresh) herbs such as red pepper flakes, bay leaves, and oregano may be added to taste. Cover the jar with a tight-fitting lid and shake to distribute the salt and herbs. Refrigerator garlic pickles will keep almost indefinitely in the refrigerator, as long as the garlic remains submerged in the vinegar.

So, now you know which tools to buy and which ones to skip, and how to deal, or not deal, with garlic breath. You have also learned how to preserve any excess garlic you may someday acquire when your infatuation for the bulb becomes a little obsessive. In the next chapter, we'll learn how to get down and dirty with garlic in the kitchen and prepare some recipes.

CHAPTER 7

Cooking With Garlic

Tomatoes and oregano make it Italian; wine and tarragon make it French.
Sour cream makes it Russian; lemon and cinnamon make it Greek.
Soy sauce makes it Chinese; garlic makes it good.

—ALICE MAY BROCK, OWNER OF ALICE'S RESTAURANT

The recipes in this book were designed to be easy, practical, healthy, and delicious. Many of them have been a part of my regular fare for years, which to me is proof that they are both good and doable. With today's hectic schedules, a recipe that is too complicated or too time consuming will not be useful to anyone, myself included. Therefore, most of these recipes can be prepared quite easily and quickly. But as I have said elsewhere in this book, their success depends on using fresh, high quality ingredients.

Try to use filtered water in these recipes. Cooking kills bacteria, but it does not remove most environmental pollutants. Very fresh, seasonal produce is a must, and organic is preferred. Also, please try to always use organic dairy products, eggs, chicken, and turkey. Not only do they taste better, but they are less apt to be contaminated with residual enviromental pollutants, hormones, and antibiotics. The treatment of the animals in organic farms tends to be more humane than in industrial farms, which is another important consideration. If you prefer to avoid animal products, you can substitute plain soymilk for dairy milk and soy cheese for any dairy cheese except chevre and feta. If you buy salmon, make sure to buy wild, not farmed. It should say if it is wild on the label.

You may have to do a little searching-around to find high-quality ingredients. Health food stores and farmers markets are good places to look for organic ingredients. You can also find organic foods at online markets. A few of the ingredients used in these recipes may not be available in all supermarkets. They include tamari soy sauce (which is infinitely better than cheap supermarket soy sauce), miso, tahini, quinoa, whole-wheat pastry flour, whole-grain pastas, and specialty types of organic brown rice. When buying miso, choose a light color, since it will be milder. When buying whole-wheat pastry flour, make sure the bag says "pastry." If it does not, the flour will be too heavy for anything except bread. For the bread recipes, use regular, organic whole-wheat flour, not whole-wheat pastry flour.

There are many types of whole-grain pastas. I favor an organic whole-wheat pasta imported from Italy and sold under the brand name of Bionature. Whole-grain pastas take a few minutes longer to cook than white-flour pastas, but they are much healthier, offering "good carbs," fiber, and more protein, vitamins, and minerals. Make sure to follow the manufacturer's directions when cooking them. If you cannot tolerate wheat, use pastas made from lentils, corn, rice, or quinoa. Try several until you find one that you like. If you are not accustomed to shopping for these products, you may be surprised at how easy to use and delicious they are in these recipes. They will all make tasty additions to your kitchen.

APPETIZERS, HORS D'OEUVRES, AND DIPS

Garlic is a traditional ingredient in many of the ethnic dishes that seem to have become standard fare for entertaining, such as hummus and guacamole. You will find some of these old favorites here, but with interesting new twists, as well as some of my own party favorites.

Garlic is the perfect guest at any dinner party. It helps to whet the appetite and break the ice. It is always noticed, always commented upon, and—as long as your guests are not dull, prudish types—always loved.

CILANTRO PESTO

If you like cilantro, this easy and delicious recipe is a must-try. It is sometimes called "chelation pesto" because two of its principal ingredients, cilantro and garlic, are reputed to help detoxify the body of heavy metals. All you are said to need is two teaspoons per day. When cilantro is in season, you can make up a large batch of this pesto and freeze it in small containers for later use.

Yield: About 1 cup

2 cups lightly packed, coarsely chopped fresh cilantro

1 cup walnuts

1/4 cup flax or olive oil

1–3 cloves garlic

1/4 teaspoon sea salt, or to taste

Pinch ascorbic acid powder, for color retention (optional)

1/4 cup dulse flakes (optional)*

1. Place the cilantro and walnuts in a food processor. While processing, add the oil, garlic, salt, and ascorbic acid through the opening in the lid. Process until the mixture is well blended. If necessary, stop the machine and scrape the sides of the container with a rubber spatula to make sure all the ingredients are processed.
2. Transfer the mixture to a small bowl. Add the dulse, if desired, and mix well. Serve as a spread on bread or spooned over pasta.

*Dulse is a sea vegetable and an excellent source of minerals. If you have never tried it but would like to, this pesto is a good recipe with which to do so. Dulse is salty, however, so you may want to add less sea salt to the recipe if you use dulse. If you do not use dulse, you may want to add more salt.

BABA GANOUSH

Yield: About 1½ cups

- 1 medium-size eggplant
- ¼ cup tahini
- 2 tablespoons lemon juice, or to taste
- 1 tablespoon olive oil
- ½ teaspoon sea salt
- 1–3 cloves garlic, pressed
- 1 tablespoon minced fresh parsley for garnish
- Paprika for garnish

Garlicky and good, this recipe is a party and potluck favorite.

1. Pierce the eggplant all over with a fork. Place on a baking sheet and bake in a preheated 400°F oven for 40 minutes, or until soft and shriveled. Set aside to cool.
2. When the eggplant is cool enough to handle, scoop out the flesh and discard the skin. Chop or mash the eggplant into small pieces. For a smooth texture, process in a blender or food processor.
3. Place the eggplant in a medium-size bowl. Add the tahini, lemon juice, oil, salt, and garlic, and mix well. Serve chilled or at room temperature with a sprinkle of parsley and a dusting of paprika.

BLACK BEAN HUMMUS

Yield: About 2 cups

- 2 cups cooked and drained black beans
- ¼ cup tahini
- 1 tablespoon tamari soy sauce, or to taste
- 1 tablespoon balsamic vinegar
- ½ teaspoon ground cumin
- 1–3 cloves garlic
- Dash cayenne pepper
- Paprika for garnish

For an unusual twist to a traditional Middle Eastern meal, serve this hummus on a bed of salad greens accompanied by Quinoa Tabouli (page 154) and Sesame, Poppy Seed, and Garlic Pita Points (page 145).

1. Place all the ingredients except the paprika in a blender or food processor and process until the mixture is smooth and creamy. Stop the machine and scrape the sides of the container with a rubber spatula, if necessary, to make sure all the ingredients are processed.
2. Sprinkle with paprika and serve at room temperature with whole-grain pita, chips, or crudités.

ROASTED GARLIC

2 large bulbs garlic

1 teaspoon olive oil

This is a garlic lover's dream—a whole bulb of roasted garlic to do with whatever you wish. See page 130 for some tempting suggestions

1. Peel the loose outer paper from the garlic bulbs and cut about 1/4 inch off the tops to expose some of the cloves. Drizzle each bulb with 1/2 teaspoon of oil.
2. Place the bulbs in a terracotta garlic roaster or wrap them in aluminum foil. Bake in a preheated 350°F oven for 45–60 minutes, or until the garlic is soft. Note that it takes a little longer to bake garlic in a terracotta garlic roaster than in foil.
3. Serve the garlic immediately, either from the roaster or arranged on a plate. To release the cloves, simply squeeze them from their wrappers. Squeeze any leftover cloves into a small covered container and refrigerate up to a few days.

VARIATION

If you prefer to roast the cloves individually, separate them from the raw bulb and arrange on a sheet of aluminum foil. Drizzle with the oil and fold the foil around them to form a closed pouch. Bake in a preheated 350°F oven for about 20–30 minutes, or until soft.

Ten Ways to Use Roasted Garlic

1. Add to almost any soup, especially blender soups that contain potatoes.
2. Stir into cooked rice, beans, and vegetables.
3. Add to mashed potatoes.
4. Add to salad dressings, dips, and spreads.
5. Spread on bread and top with fresh mozzarella and a slice of tomato.
6. Spread on pizza dough before adding the other ingredients.
7. Mix with butter and spread on grilled corn-on-the-cob.
8. Mix with a little olive oil and toss with cooked pasta just before serving.
9. Add to a white sauce.
10. Mix with sour cream and serve over baked potatoes.

OLIVE, ALMOND, AND GARLIC PÂTÉ

This pâté is sometimes mistaken for liver pâté.

YIELD: 6–12 SERVINGS

1 cup pitted black olives, drained
1 cup water
1/2 cup almonds
10 cloves garlic
1/4 cup whole-wheat pastry flour
1–2 tablespoons tamari soy sauce
1/2 teaspoon dried thyme
1/2 teaspoon dried sage
1/4 teaspoon pepper, or to taste
2 tablespoons parsley, chives, or garlic grass

1. Place all the ingredients except the parsley, in a blender or food processor and process on low speed until very smooth. Stop the machine and scrape the sides of the container with a rubber spatula, if necessary, to make sure all the ingredients are processed.
2. Lightly grease and flour an 8-inch cake pan. Pour the mixture into the pan and bake in a preheated 350°F oven for 45 minutes, or until set. Place in the refrigerator to chill for at least 2 hours. Cover if it will be refrigerated for an extended period.
3. To serve, cut the pâté into little squares or diamonds and garnish with a sprinkling of parsley. Accompany with hot, crusty whole-grain bread or crackers.

GARLICKY PARTY NUTS

Curry spices and garlic make these nuts an irresistible and healthy snack.

YIELD: 2½ CUPS

- 1 cup walnuts
- 1 cup almonds
- ½ cup pumpkin seeds
- 2 tablespoons tamari soy sauce, or to taste
- 1 teaspoon ground cumin
- ½ teaspoon turmeric
- ½ teaspoon ground cardamom
- ⅛ teaspoon cayenne pepper, or to taste
- 10–12 cloves garlic, pressed

1. Combine the walnuts and almonds in a large bowl. Cover with water and let soak for 10 minutes. (This step will help the spices adhere to the nuts.)
2. Place the pumpkin seeds in a separate bowl. Cover with water and let soak for 10 minutes.
3. Drain the nuts, dry the bowl, and return the nuts to the bowl. Add the remaining ingredients and mix well.
4. Using a slotted spoon, remove the nuts from the bowl and arrange on a baking sheet. Bake in a preheated 350°F oven for 5 minutes.
5. Drain the pumpkin seeds and place in the bowl with the remaining spice mixture. Stir to coat, then add to the roasting nuts. Bake 5 minutes, or until the nuts and seeds are dry and lightly toasted.

BRUSCHETTA WITH ROASTED GARLIC TAPENADE

This variation of a basic tapenade features salty kalamata olives and piquant capers.

YIELD: ABOUT ½ CUP

- 1 cup pitted kalamata olives
- 2 tablespoons olive oil
- 2 tablespoons mashed roasted garlic
- 1 tablespoon capers
- ½ teaspoon dried thyme
- Pinch cayenne (optional)

1. Place all the ingredients in a blender or food processor and process just until blended. The tapenade should not be completely smooth.
2. Serve as a dip with crackers. Store any leftover tapenade in a covered container in the refrigerator.

ROASTED RED PEPPER–GARLIC DIP

YIELD: ABOUT 1½ CUPS

1 red bell pepper

1 package (10 ounces) firm silken tofu (I use Mori-Nu brand)

2 tablespoons white or yellow miso

1½ tablespoons mashed roasted garlic

1 teaspoon paprika

½ teaspoon dried basil

Pinch cayenne pepper (optional)

This dip has a rich yet mild flavor. It can also be thinned with a little filtered water and used as a sauce.

1. Place the bell pepper on a cookie sheet under a preheated broiler about 5 minutes, or until charred on top. Turn over and broil another 3–5 minutes, or until the other side is charred.
2. Remove the pepper and immediately place in a bowl. Cover the bowl with a plate and let the pepper steam for 20 minutes, or until its skin has loosened.
3. When the pepper is cool enough to handle, carefully peel off the charred skin. It should come off easily. Cut the pepper in half and remove the seeds. Cut the halves into strips and place in a blender or food processor along with the remaining ingredients. Process until smooth and creamy. Stop the machine and scrape the sides of the container with a rubber spatula, if necessary, to make sure all the ingredients are processed.
4. Serve as a dip with crackers or crudités, or add a dollop to pasta, baked potatoes, or cooked vegetables.

VARIATION

This recipe also makes an excellent sauce. Thin it with a little filtered water and gently heat, but do not boil. You may also need to adjust the seasonings.

TAHINI-CARROT SPREAD

Don't let the "health food store" ingredients keep you from trying this tasty and easy-to-prepare spread. I have made it for years, and it is always well received. Even my five-year-old nephew, who is accustomed to standard American fare, likes it stuffed into whole-wheat pita bread.

Yield: About 1 cup

- 1/2 cup tahini
- 2 tablespoons water
- 1 tablespoon balsamic vinegar
- 1 tablespoon tamari soy sauce
- 1 cup finely grated carrots*
- 1/4 cup nutritional yeast flakes (optional)**
- 3 cloves garlic, pressed, or to taste

1. In a medium-size bowl, combine the tahini, water, vinegar, and tamari; mix with a fork until thick and creamy.
2. Add the remaining ingredients and mix again. If the spread is too dry, add another tablespoon of water. Serve as a spread in sandwiches or on crackers.

*The carrot needs to be grated by hand. A food processor will not grate it finely enough. Most four-sided hand graters have grating surfaces in two sizes. It may take a minute longer, but using the fine side will make this spread come out best.

**Nutritional yeast gives this spread a much richer taste.

WHITE BEAN PURÉE

This simple purée is a nice change from hummus. Try it with Sesame, Poppy Seed, and Garlic Pita Points (page 145) or Garlic-Parmesan Rice Cakes (page 163).

Yield: About 2 cups

- 2 cups cooked and drained Great Northern beans
- 2 tablespoons olive oil
- 1/4 teaspoon sea salt, or to taste
- 1 tablespoon mashed roasted garlic
- 1 tablespoon balsamic vinegar
- 1/2 teaspoon dried sage

1. Place all the ingredients in a food processor and process until smooth. Stop the machine and scrape the sides of the container with a rubber spatula, if necessary, to make sure all the ingredients are processed.
2. Serve as a dip or spread, or as a salad over a bed of fresh greens.

SOUPS

In traditional Chinese medicine, garlic is a warming food, which makes a steaming bowl of garlic soup the perfect comfort food on a cold winter's day. But don't reserve these soups for winter only. Any cool or rainy day is perfect to enjoy their richly flavored goodness. Although all of these soups contain large amounts of garlic, you may be surprised at how distinctive each one is.

GARLIC-LENTIL SOUP

YIELD: 4 SERVINGS

- 1 cup dry green lentils
- 2 tablespoons olive oil
- 3 cups chopped sweet onion
- 6 bay leaves
- 4 sprigs fresh rosemary (optional)
- 12 cloves garlic, sliced
- 4–5 cups water
- 2 tablespoons red wine or balsamic vinegar
- 2 tablespoons tamari soy sauce, or to taste
- Dash cayenne pepper or hot sauce, or to taste

Simple and hearty.

1. Pick through the lentils to remove any dirt, stones, or damaged legumes, then wash and drain. Set aside.
2. Heat the oil in a large, heavy kettle such as a cast-iron Dutch oven. Add the onion, bay leaves, and rosemary, and sauté over medium-low heat for 10 minutes. Add the garlic and sauté for 10 minutes more.
3. Place the lentils, water, and vinegar in the pot with the onions and garlic, and cover. Bring to a boil, then reduce the heat and simmer, stirring occasionally, for about 40 minutes, or until the lentils are tender.
4. Add the tamari and simmer slowly, stirring occasionally, about 20–30 minutes more, or until the broth becomes rich and thick. If it becomes too thick, add more water.
5. Before serving, add the cayenne pepper. Enjoy with fresh whole-grain bread and a salad.

GARLICKY CHICKEN SOUP

This is Grandma's chicken soup with the oomph of garlic and a subtle Asian flair.

Yield: 6 servings

Stock

3-pound chicken, cut up

2 stalks celery

1 medium carrot

1 medium onion

12 cloves garlic

6 bay leaves

6 cups water

Soup

4 carrots, chopped

3 stalks celery, chopped

1 cup chopped onion

6 cloves garlic, sliced

1/4 cup dry white wine (optional)

3 tablespoons tamari soy sauce, or to taste

1/4 teaspoon Chinese five spice powder

1 cup fresh bean sprouts

1/4 cup chopped scallions

Dash cayenne pepper (optional)

1. To prepare the stock, place the chicken in a large kettle along with the remaining stock ingredients. (You do not need to chop the veggies.) Bring to a boil, then reduce the heat and simmer for 1 hour, or until the chicken is cooked. Remove the chicken and vegetables from the kettle. Place the vegetables in a blender and set the chicken on a platter to cool.
2. To make the soup, pour the stock into a large bowl. Skim off about 2–3 tablespoons of fat, then return the stock to the kettle. Add the chopped carrots, celery, and onion, and the sliced garlic. Simmer over medium heat for 10–15 minutes, or until the vegetables are tender.
3. Ladle enough of the stock into the blender to purée the vegetables that were used to make the stock. Add the puréed vegetables to the kettle along with the remaining stock.
4. When the chicken is cool enough to handle, pick the meat off the bones. You should have about 3 cups. Add the meat to the kettle along with the wine, tamari, and five spice powder. Bring to a boil, then reduce the heat and simmer, covered, for 15 minutes.
5. Add the bean sprouts and scallions, and simmer, uncovered, for 1 minute. Add the cayenne, if desired. Serve with whole-grain bread and a green salad.

BABY LIMA BEAN SOUP WITH ROSEMARY AND GARLIC

YIELD: 8 SERVINGS

2 cups dry baby lima beans

5 cups water or vegetable stock

1 large onion, chopped

2 stalks celery, chopped

2 medium carrots, sliced

1/4 cup tamari soy sauce

1 tablespoon balsamic vinegar

6 sprigs fresh rosemary, or 2 teaspoons dried

1/4 cup tahini

3 cloves garlic, pressed, or to taste

Pinch cayenne pepper, or to taste

This hearty soup is creamy and rich.

1. Pick through the beans to remove any dirt, stones, or damaged beans, then wash and drain. Place in a large bowl and add enough water to cover by approximately 2 inches. Allow to soak about 8 hours.

2. Drain and rinse the soaked beans. Place in a large, heavy kettle such as a cast-iron Dutch oven and add 5 cups water. Cover and bring to a boil over high heat. Reduce the heat to a gentle simmer and cook about 1 hour, or until the beans are tender.

3. Add the onion, celery, carrots, tamari, vinegar, and rosemary, and continue to simmer about 30 minutes, or until the vegetables are tender.

4. Add the tahini and mix well. Bring to a boil and stir until the broth thickens. Remove from the heat and add the garlic and cayenne. Serve with whole-grain bread and a salad.

GARLIC, GREENS, AND RICE SOUP

Collard greens combined with garlic and sun-dried tomatoes make this delectable soup as healthy as it is delicious.

Yield: 6 servings

- 2 tablespoons olive oil
- 1 large Spanish onion, chopped (about 2 cups)
- 12 cloves garlic, minced
- 4 bay leaves
- 2 cups chopped collard greens, firmly packed
- 5 cups water
- 1½ cups cooked brown basmati rice
- 20 sun-dried tomato halves, cut into pieces with scissors
- ¼ cup tamari soy sauce
- 3 sprigs fresh rosemary, or 1 teaspoon dried
- 1 teaspoon dried basil

1. Heat the oil in a large, heavy kettle such as a cast-iron Dutch oven. Add the onion, garlic, and bay leaves, and sauté very slowly over low heat, for at least 30 minutes, stirring occasionally.
2. Raise the heat to high and add the collard greens. Sauté until wilted, then add the remaining ingredients. Bring to a boil, then reduce the heat and simmer, stirring occasionally, for 30 minutes, or until the collards and rice are tender. Serve with homemade cornbread.

Using Garlic Scallions, Scapes, and Chives

Garlic in every stage of its growth is still garlic and has all its wonderfully pungent qualities. Therefore, garlic scallions, scapes, and chives can be substituted for garlic cloves in most of these recipes. About the only thing that you can't do with garlic scallions, scapes, or chives is press them or use them in recipes that require long, slow cooking.

Garlic scallions and scapes can be chopped, stir-fried, or lightly sautéed in any dish in which garlic cloves would normally be used. They can also be added raw to salads. Garlic chives, sometimes called garlic grass, can be chopped and sprinkled raw on any cooked dish or salad in which a garlic taste is desired.

POTATO AND CAULIFLOWER SOUP WITH ROASTED GARLIC

YIELD: 6–8 SMALL SERVINGS

- 4 cups peeled and cubed baking potatoes
- 3½–4 cups cauliflower flowerets (about 1 small head)
- 1 cup chopped sweet onion
- 1 teaspoon sea salt
- 1½–2½ cups water
- 2 cups milk
- 2 tablespoons mashed roasted garlic
- 1 tablespoon chopped fresh tarragon, or ½ teaspoon dried
- ⅛ teaspoon white pepper, or to taste

This soup has a mild but rich flavor, making it an easy first course for a dinner party. I make it in a pressure cooker, but you can also use a regular soup pot.

1. Place the potatoes, cauliflower, onion, and salt in a pressure cooker along with 1½ cups of the water. Cover and cook over high heat until the pressure comes up. Remove the cooker from the heat and let the pressure come down on its own. If making this soup in a Dutch oven or soup pot, bring 2½ cups of water, the potatoes, cauliflower, onion, and salt to a boil. Reduce the heat to medium and simmer for 20 minutes, or until the vegetables are tender. Add more water, if necessary, to keep the vegetables from sticking or burning.
2. When the vegetables are tender, add the milk, roasted garlic, tarragon, and white pepper. Using a handheld blender, regular blender, or food processor, process the soup until smooth and creamy. If using a blender or food processor, you may have to do this in two or more batches. Add more milk if the soup is too thick and adjust the seasonings.
3. Serve immediately with fresh whole-grain bread.

POTATO AND MUSTARD GREENS SOUP WITH ROASTED GARLIC

Green and garlicky with a hearty earthiness.

Yield: 4–6 servings

- 1 1/2 pounds potatoes (about 4 medium), cut into chunks
- 4 cups coarsely chopped mustard greens
- 1 onion, cut into chunks
- 1 teaspoon sea salt, or to taste
- 4 bay leaves
- 1/3 cup dry white wine
- 1–2 cups water
- 2 cups milk
- 2 tablespoons mashed roasted garlic
- 1/4 teaspoon white pepper, or to taste
- Minced fresh parsley for garnish

1. Place the potatoes, mustard greens, onion, salt, and bay leaves in a pressure cooker along with the wine and 1 cup water. Cover and cook over high heat until the pressure comes up. Remove the cooker from the heat and let the pressure come down on its own. If the potatoes and vegetables are not done, cook a few minutes more. If making this soup in a Dutch oven or soup pot, bring 2 cups of water, the potatoes, mustard greens, onion, and bay leaves to a boil. Reduce the heat to medium and simmer for 30 minutes, or until the ingredients are tender. Add more water, if necessary, to keep the vegetables from sticking or burning.
2. When the ingredients are cooked, remove and discard the bay leaves. Add the milk and roasted garlic. Using a handheld blender, regular blender, or food processor, process the soup until smooth. If using a blender or food processor, you may have to do this in two or more batches. Add more milk if the soup is too thick. Stir in the white pepper.
3. Reheat if desired, but do not boil. Garnish with parsley and serve with whole-grain sourdough rolls.

SOUP PROVENÇAL

YIELD: 4 SERVINGS

1–2 tablespoons olive oil

1 medium onion, sliced

4 bay leaves

2 bulbs garlic, peeled and chopped

4 cups water or vegetable stock

1 large potato, scrubbed and diced

½ teaspoon dried thyme

¼ cup miso

Pinch cayenne pepper, or to taste

I have made this soup for years. It is a favorite with my cooking students and great if you have a cold.

1. Heat the oil in a large, heavy kettle such as a cast-iron Dutch oven. Add the onion and bay leaves, and sauté over low heat for 5–10 minutes, or until the onion is translucent. Add the garlic. Sauté for 10–15 minutes more, or until the onions are browned.
2. Add the water, potato, and thyme. Bring the mixture to a boil, then reduce the heat and simmer, covered, for 15 minutes, or until the potato is tender.
3. Place the miso in a small bowl. Add about ½ cup of the soup broth and stir until the miso is dissolved. Add the dissolved miso to the soup along with the cayenne.
4. Reheat, if desired, but do not boil. Serve with a loaf of sourdough whole-grain bread, goats' milk cheese, and a green salad for a delicious peasant-style meal.

VARIATION

Substitute tamari soy sauce to taste for the miso.

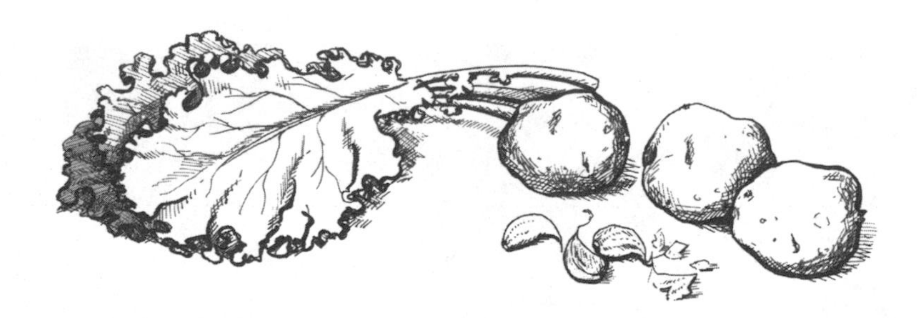

GAZPACHO SUPREME

This gazpacho is made with a juice extractor. The addition of carrots mellows the tomatoes and imparts a luscious sweetness. Make sure all the vegetables are chilled before you begin, and serve this refreshing, cold soup as soon as possible after it is made. People have told me that this is the best gazpacho they have ever tasted.

YIELD: 6 SERVINGS

4 medium tomatoes (or enough for 3 cups juice)

3 cloves garlic

4 medium carrots (or enough for 2 cups juice)

1 medium cucumber, grated

½ green bell pepper, finely chopped

2 tablespoons chopped fresh basil, or 1 teaspoon dried

1 tablespoon red wine vinegar or lemon juice

Sea salt to taste

1. Core the tomatoes and run them through a juice extractor, saving the pulp. Transfer both the juice and the pulp to a large bowl. Note that it is important to juice the tomatoes before the carrots because you do not want to mix the tomato pulp, which you will be using, with the carrot pulp, which you will be discarding.
2. Run the garlic through the juicer. It is not necessary to peel it first.
3. Juice the carrots and add the carrot-garlic juice to the tomatoes.
4. Mix in the remaining ingredients and serve immediately with Sesame, Poppy Seed, and Garlic Pita Points (page 145).

BREADS AND PIZZA

What better medium for garlic to show off its talents than hot, freshly baked whole-grain breads and pizza? These recipes are particularly easy to make if you have a bread machine. If you have one stashed away that you don't use, dust it off and put it on your kitchen counter because you will want to make these recipes often. They are so delicious that they may even help you convince your favorite white bread lover to go for something healthier.

DONNA'S GARLIC BREAD

YIELD: 6 SERVINGS

1 long baguette French bread, unsliced (I like to use whole-grain pain de campagne)

½ cup butter

6 cloves garlic, minced or pressed

Donna Metcalfe, owner of Good Scents, an online aromatherapy boutique (www.goodscents.org), is a garlic lover with passion. This recipe is her favorite way of making garlic bread because the loaf stays warm, soft, and very garlicky.

1. Slice the bread in 1-inch slices, making sure not to cut all the way through the bottom to leave the slices attached.
2. Place the butter and garlic in a small saucepan over low heat. Stir until the butter is melted and the mixture is well combined and fragrant.
3. Gently separate the slices of bread but be careful to keep them attached. Spoon 1–2 teaspoons of the garlic-butter mixture over each slice, making sure to include some bits of garlic on each slice. Spoon any remaining garlic butter over the top. Wrap the loaf in foil, sealing it tightly, and bake in a preheated 250°F oven for 15–20 minutes, or until warmed through. Serve hot.

GARLIC-ROSEMARY FOCACCIA

Use a bread machine to mix and knead the dough for this flavorful bread.

Yield: 1 flat loaf

Dough

1½ cups plus 2 tablespoons whole-wheat flour

1 cup water

¼ cup vital wheat gluten*

2 tablespoons olive oil

1 tablespoon dry active yeast

1 tablespoon raw sugar

½ teaspoon sea salt

Topping

12 cloves garlic, pressed

2 tablespoons olive oil

1 tablespoon finely minced fresh rosemary

½ teaspoon sea salt

1. Place all the dough ingredients in a bread machine and process until the dough has risen once. If you do not have a bread machine, mix together all the dough ingredients in a large bowl and knead by hand for at least 10 minutes. Cover the bowl with a towel and let the dough rise for about 1 hour in a warm place.
2. When the dough has doubled in bulk, remove it from the machine and flatten it onto an oiled 11-x-16-inch cookie sheet. It is not necessary for the dough to completely cover the cookie sheet.
3. In a small bowl, mix together the topping ingredients and spread over the dough. Let the dough rise, uncovered or lightly covered with a damp dish towel, for about 30 minutes in a warm place.
4. Place the dough in a cold oven, then turn the heat to 350°F and bake for 10 minutes, or until golden brown on the top and bottom.
5. Cut into squares and serve warm. Leftover slices can be frozen; to reheat, let thaw, then toast briefly.

*Vital wheat gluten is a wonderful addition to whole-grain breads because it helps them rise and attain a pleasingly light texture. It can be purchased at natural food stores.

BASIC BRUSCHETTA

YIELD: 6 SERVINGS

3 medium ripe tomatoes

1 baguette, preferably whole-grain

2 tablespoons olive oil, or as needed

2 cloves garlic

2 tablespoons chopped fresh basil

Sea salt to taste

Among the more popular items served at Italian restaurants today is bruschetta, especially when made with large chunks of vine-ripened tomatoes. This recipe is the one I serve guests in my home when I have fresh vine-ripened tomatoes on hand.

1. To peel the tomatoes, first drop them into a large pot of boiling water for about 3 seconds. Remove with a slotted spoon.
2. When the tomatoes are cool enough to handle, remove the skin, then seed, chop, and place in a colander over a bowl to catch juice. Let drain about 30 minutes. Save the juice for another use.
3. Cut the baguette into ½-inch-thick slices and brush both sides with oil. Place the bread slices under a preheated broiler until toasted, then turn and toast the other side. Rub the toasted slices with the garlic cloves.
4. Transfer the chopped tomatoes to a medium-size bowl. Add the basil and salt, and stir carefully to combine. To serve, arrange the toasted bread on a serving platter and top with the tomato mixture.

VARIATION

Spread 2 bulbs of roasted garlic on the toasted bread instead of rubbing them with raw garlic.

SESAME, POPPY SEED, AND GARLIC PITA POINTS

Crisp and garlicky, these pita points are perfect for scooping up your favorite dip.

Yield: 48 points

6 whole-grain pita rounds

12 cloves garlic, pressed, or to taste

1/4 cup olive oil

2 tablespoons sesame seeds

1 tablespoon poppy seeds

1. Cut the pita loaves in half and carefully split them open. This will give you 24 half-moon-shaped pieces.
2. Combine the garlic and oil in a cup or small bowl and brush over the insides of the split pieces. Be careful not to use up all of the garlic-oil mixture on the first few pieces. Cut each half-moon piece into 4 pie-shaped wedges.
3. Place the pita pieces on unoiled cookie sheets with the oil sides up. Sprinkle half with poppy seeds and the other half with sesame seeds. Place under a preheated 400°F broiler for about 4 minutes, or until toasty brown and crisp. Be careful not to burn. If some are still a little soft, put them back under the hot broiler with the heat off.
4. Allow the points to cool, then serve with your favorite dip. Leftovers can be stored in a plastic bag up to 24 hours.

GARLIC TOAST FOR TWO

Quick and delicious, this recipe is perfect for an informal at-home meal.

Yield: 2 servings

6 cloves garlic, pressed

1 tablespoon olive oil

Pinch sea salt

2 thick slices whole-grain bread

1. Combine the garlic, oil, and salt in a cup or small bowl. Brush over the bread slices.
2. Place the bread slices on a cookie sheet under a preheated broiler for about 2 minutes, or until toasty brown. Serve hot with soup or salad.

ARTICHOKE, GARLIC, AND FRESH TOMATO PIZZA

YIELD: 1 PIZZA

Dough

1 1/2 cups plus 2 tablespoons whole-wheat flour

1 cup water

1/4 cup vital wheat gluten*

2 tablespoons olive oil

1 tablespoon dry active yeast

1 tablespoon raw sugar

1/2 teaspoon sea salt

Topping

6–12 cloves garlic, pressed

1 tablespoon olive oil

1 teaspoon dried basil

1/2 teaspoon dried oregano

1/2 teaspoon sea salt

1 can (16 ounces) artichoke hearts, drained and finely chopped

3–4 tomatoes

1/2 cup freshly grated mozzarella

1/4 cup freshly grated Parmesan cheese

If you use a bread machine to make the dough, this pizza will take you just a few minutes to throw together.

1. Place all the dough ingredients in a bread machine and process until the dough has risen once. If you do not have a bread machine, mix together all the dough ingredients in a large bowl and knead by hand for at least 10 minutes. Cover the bowl with a towel and let the dough rise for about 1 hour in a warm place.
2. After the dough has risen, turn it out onto a well-oiled 11-x-16-inch cookie sheet. Pat and stretch the dough to cover the bottom and sides of the sheet.
3. Press the garlic into a medium-size bowl. Add the oil, herbs, and salt, and stir to combine. Add the artichoke hearts and mix well.
4. Cut the tomatoes into slices 1/4–1/2 inch thick. Select the 12 biggest slices and set aside.
5. Spread the artichoke mixture evenly over the crust. Arrange the tomato slices in a layer over the artichoke mixture. Top with the grated cheeses. Place the pizza in a cold oven, then turn the heat to 375°F. Bake the pizza for 12 minutes, or until the crust is crispy and golden brown. (Lift the edge of the pizza to check the underside.)
6. To serve, cut the pizza into 12 squares, with 1 tomato slice per piece. Serve hot.

*Vital wheat gluten is a wonderful addition to whole-grain breads because it helps them rise and attain a pleasingly light texture. It can be purchased at natural food stores.

ONION AND GARLIC PIZZA

Caramelized onions and garlic make a scrumptious pizza topping.

Yield: 1 Pizza

Dough

1½ cups plus 2 tablespoons whole-wheat flour

1 cup water

¼ cup vital wheat gluten*

2 tablespoons olive oil

1 tablespoon dry active yeast

1 tablespoon raw sugar

½ teaspoon sea salt

Topping

2 tablespoons olive oil

2 large Spanish onions, sliced (about 4 cups)

Cloves from 1 garlic bulb, peeled and sliced

2 teaspoons herbes de Provence

1 teaspoon sea salt

White pepper to taste

1. Place all the dough ingredients in a bread machine and process until the dough has risen once. If you do not have a bread machine, mix together all the dough ingredients in a large bowl and knead by hand for at least 10 minutes. Cover the bowl with a towel and let the dough rise for about 1 hour in a warm place.
2. Heat the oil in a large skillet. Add the onions and sauté over low heat for about 10 minutes. Add the garlic and sauté very slowly for about 20 minutes, or until the onions are reduced by half. Add the herbes de Provence, salt, and pepper, and stir to combine. Set aside to cool.
3. After the dough has risen, turn it out onto a well-oiled 11-x-16-inch cookie sheet. Pat and stretch the dough to cover the bottom and sides of the sheet.
4. When the onion-garlic mixture has cooled, spread it evenly over the crust. Place the pizza in a cold oven, then turn the heat to 375°F. Bake the pizza about 10 minutes, or until the crust is crispy and golden brown. (Lift the edge of the pizza to check the underside.)
5. Cut into 12 slices and serve as a main course with soup or a salad, or cut into small squares and serve as a party appetizer.

*Vital wheat gluten is a wonderful addition to whole-grain breads because it helps them rise and attain a pleasingly light texture. It can be purchased at natural food stores.

SAUCES AND SALAD DRESSINGS

Flavorful garlic-rich sauces and salad dressings can be a cook's best resources. They have the power to transform plain-Jane dishes into sensuous and luscious delights without a lot of fuss or work. Be creative with your use of these sauces and dressings. Don't reserve the salad dressings for cold salads only. Try them over hot steamed vegetables instead of the usual seasonings. And use the sauces to top different combinations of pasta or grain and vegetable dishes.

ROASTED GARLIC AND BELL PEPPER DRESSING

YIELD: ABOUT 1 CUP

1 bell pepper

1/2 cup olive oil

2 tablespoons balsamic vinegar

1 tablespoon mashed roasted garlic

1 tablespoon chopped fresh basil, or 1 teaspoon dried

1/2 teaspoon sea salt

This dressing has a pretty color and a rich, slightly sweet flavor.

1. Place the bell pepper on a cookie sheet under a preheated broiler about 5 minutes, or until charred on top. Turn over and broil another 3–5 minutes, or until the other side is charred.
2. Remove the pepper and immediately place in a bowl. Cover the bowl with a plate and let the pepper steam for 20 minutes, or until its skin has loosened.
3. When the pepper is cool enough to handle, carefully peel off the charred skin. It should come off easily. Cut the pepper in half and remove the seeds. Cut the halves into strips and place in a blender, along with the remaining ingredients. Process until smooth. Stop the machine and scrape the sides of the container with a rubber spatula, if necessary, to make sure all the ingredients are processed.
4. Serve over a green salad or cooked vegetables. Refrigerate any leftover dressing in a covered jar.

CREAMY GARLIC-MISO DRESSING

The freshness of lime and the nuttiness of flax combine beautifully with garlic and miso for a deliciously uncommon dressing. When you serve this dressing, you are sure to be asked how to make it.

YIELD: ABOUT 3/4 CUP

- 1/2 cup flax or olive oil
- 1/4 cup lime juice, lemon juice, or rice vinegar
- 2 teaspoons miso*
- 1–3 cloves garlic
- Basil or tarragon to taste (optional)

1. Place all the ingredients in a blender and process until creamy. Stop the machine and scrape the sides of the container with a rubber spatula, if necessary, to make sure all the ingredients are processed.
2. Serve over a green salad or cooked vegetables. Refrigerate any leftover dressing in a covered jar.

*You can use any type of miso except hatcho miso, which is too strong for this recipe. I prefer yellow or white miso.

QUICK TAHINI-GARLIC SAUCE

This easy, no-cook, protein-rich sauce livens up grain, pasta, and rice dishes.

YIELD: ABOUT 1 CUP

- 1/2 cup tahini
- 5 tablespoons water
- 1 tablespoon plus 1 teaspoon tamari soy sauce
- 1 tablespoon balsamic vinegar
- 1 clove garlic, pressed

1. Place the tahini in a small bowl and gradually stir in the water. Add the tamari, vinegar, and garlic. Whip with a fork until well blended.
2. Serve over vegetable-topped quinoa, rice, or whole-grain pasta.

VARIATION

Substitute sea salt to taste for the tamari, and lemon for the balsamic vinegar. The sauce will still be quite good, although the taste will not be quite as rich.

GARLIC BUTTER

YIELD: 1/2 POUND BUTTER

- 2 sticks butter, softened
- 12 cloves garlic, pressed, or to taste
- 1/4 cup finely minced fresh parsley
- Pinch sea salt (optional)

Keep some garlic butter in the freezer to use whenever you need a bit of decadently delicious seasoning.

1. In a large bowl, combine the butter with the remaining ingredients. Turn the mixture onto a sheet of waxed paper and, using your hands and the paper, shape it into a log.
2. To use the butter, slice off pieces to spread on bread or to season vegetables. To store, wrap the log in waxed paper, place in a freezer bag or plastic wrap, and store in the freezer.

AÏOLI

YIELD: ABOUT 1 CUP

- 6 cloves garlic
- 2 egg yolks, from very fresh organic eggs*
- 2 tablespoons lemon juice
- 1/2 teaspoon sea salt
- 1 cup olive oil

This classic French garlic mayonnaise can be made in a food processor, in a blender, or by hand. When made in a blender, it thickens more quickly and has a stronger flavor.

1. Place the garlic cloves in the blender along with the egg yolks, lemon juice, and salt. Process on low until smooth. Stop the machine and scrape the sides of the container with a rubber spatula, if necessary, to make sure all the ingredients are processed.
2. With the blender running, slowly drizzle in the oil. This must be done slowly or the mayonnaise will separate. Continue processing until the mayonnaise thickens. Use immediately or store in a covered jar in the refrigerator for up to 3 days.

*Although organic eggs are safer than industrially farmed eggs, all raw eggs carry the danger of salmonella. Therefore, do not serve recipes with raw eggs to the elderly, to the very young, or to persons with weak immune systems.

MANGO-GARLIC DRESSING

YIELD: ABOUT 1 1/4 CUPS

1 cup ripe mango, diced into 1/2-inch cubes

1/4 cup flax oil

1/4 cup wine vinegar

1/4 teaspoon sea salt

1 clove garlic

3 tablespoons chopped cilantro leaves

The pretty orange color of this luscious dressing is a perfect complement to garden-fresh summer greens.

1. Place the mango, oil, vinegar, salt, and garlic clove in a blender and process until smooth and creamy. Stop the machine and scrape the sides of the container with a rubber spatula, if necessary, to make sure all the ingredients are processed.
2. Serve over individual plates of salad greens and garnish with cilantro. Refrigerate any leftover dressing in a covered jar.

GARLIC-PEANUT SAUCE

YIELD: ABOUT 1 1/2 CUPS

1/2 cup natural peanut butter without added ingredients

1 1/4 cups water

1 tablespoon balsamic vinegar

2–3 cloves garlic, pressed

1/2 teaspoon sea salt, or tamari soy sauce to taste

Pinch cayenne pepper

My French husband would never eat peanut butter—until I got him to try this delicious sauce. Garlic and peanuts make perfect companions. Not only do they taste great together, garlic has been shown to destroy aflatoxin mold, which peanuts are known to sometimes harbor.

1. Place the peanut butter in a medium-size saucepan and slowly stir in the water. Cook the mixture over medium-high heat, stirring constantly with a whisk, until the sauce comes to a boil and thickens.
2. Stir in the vinegar and garlic, and remove the pan from the heat. Add the salt and cayenne pepper and mix well. For a quick and hearty meal, serve with steamed vegetables over a bed of rice, whole-grain pasta, millet, or quinoa.

LUSCIOUS TOMATO-GARLIC SAUCE

YIELD: ABOUT 2 CUPS

6 medium tomatoes
2 tablespoons olive oil
1 cup chopped onion
12 cloves garlic, sliced
6 bay leaves
1/4 cup chopped fresh basil
1/2 teaspoon sea salt

Reserve this wonderful sauce for summer, when you can get garden-fresh organic tomatoes.

1. To peel the tomatoes first drop them into a large pot of boiling water for about 3 seconds, then remove them from the water with a slotted spoon. When they are cool enough to handle, remove the skin. Chop and set aside.
2. Heat the oil in a large, heavy saucepan. Add the onion and sauté over medium-low heat for 3–4 minutes. Add the garlic and bay leaves, and sauté 5 minutes more.
3. Add the tomatoes to the pan. Bring the mixture to a boil, then reduce the heat and gently simmer about 1 hour, or until reduced by about half. Add the basil and salt, and simmer 2 minutes more. Serve over pasta or polenta.

GARLIC-FLAX DRESSING

YIELD: ABOUT 1 CUP

1/2 cup flax oil
1/4 cup balsamic vinegar
3–4 tablespoons tamari soy sauce
3 cloves garlic, pressed, or to taste
1 tablespoon chopped fresh tarragon or basil, or 1 teaspoon dried (optional)
1 teaspoon honey (optional)
1 tablespoon Dijon-style mustard (optional)

This is my standard, all-around dressing and a tasty way to get a daily dose of both flax oil and garlic. Most students in my cooking classes end up adopting it, too. This dressing is wonderful on salads, cooked vegetables, and beans.

1. Place the oil, vinegar, tamari, and garlic in a jar. Add basil, honey, and/or mustard, if desired. Screw the lid on the jar, and shake well.
2. Use on green salads or cooked vegetables. Refrigerate any leftover dressing in a covered jar.

SALADS

What is a salad without garlic? Just a boring mix of cold ingredients. Add some garlic and *voilá*! You have something worth eating. Whether you enjoy your salads before the meal or you prefer them after, *à la Français*, garlic always makes them better.

ROASTED BELL PEPPERS WITH OLIVE OIL AND GARLIC

Roasted bell peppers of all colors are versatile and delicious, although the purple ones will turn gray when roasted.

YIELD: ABOUT 1½ CUPS

4–6 bell peppers

2 tablespoons olive oil

3 cloves garlic, pressed

½ teaspoon dried basil

½ teaspoon sea salt

1. Place the bell peppers on a cookie sheet under a preheated broiler about 5 minutes, or until charred on top. Turn over and broil another 3–5 minutes, or until the other side is charred.
2. Remove the peppers and immediately place in a bowl. Cover the bowl with a plate and let the peppers steam for 20 minutes, or until their skins have loosened.
3. When the peppers are cool enough to handle, carefully peel the charred skin. It should come off easily. Cut the peppers in half, remove their seeds, and cut the halves into strips. Place in a medium-size bowl and set aside.
4. Combine the oil, garlic, basil, and salt in a cup or small bowl and pour over the peppers. Use as a salad or sandwich ingredient, or as a colorful garnish.

QUINOA TABOULI

YIELD: 4–6 SERVINGS

1 cup quinoa

2 cups water

1/4 cup lemon juice

2 tablespoons olive oil

2 tablespoons chopped fresh mint, or 1 teaspoon dried

3 cloves garlic, pressed

1/2 teaspoon sea salt

3/4 cup finely chopped fresh parsley

1/2 cup finely chopped scallions

1/2 cup finely chopped tomato (optional)

Quinoa is light and mild-flavored with a pleasant texture and lots of protein. I prefer this recipe over the traditional wheat-based tabouli.

1. Place the quinoa in a medium-size saucepan. Cover with water, swish around to wash, then drain using a wire strainer. Return the quinoa to the pan and add the 2 cups water. Cover and bring to a boil over high heat, then reduce the heat to medium-low and simmer, without stirring, for about 15–20 minutes, or until the water is absorbed.

2. Transfer the cooked quinoa to a large bowl. Add the lemon juice, oil, mint, garlic, and salt, and stir to combine. Place in the refrigerator for about 1 hour, or until chilled.

3. Add the parsley, scallions, and tomato, and mix well. Serve chilled.

GARLICKY GUACAMOLE

Garlic and avocado make a marvelous pair in this classic Mexican dish.

YIELD: 2–4 SERVINGS

1 cup mashed ripe avocado

1/2 cup finely chopped tomato

1/3 cup finely chopped green bell pepper

3 tablespoons lemon or lime juice

2 tablespoons finely minced red onion

1/2 teaspoon ground cumin

2 cloves garlic, pressed

Pinch cayenne pepper

Sea salt to taste

2 tablespoons chopped fresh cilantro for garnish

1. Place all the ingredients except the cilantro in a medium-size bowl and mix well. Taste and adjust the seasonings.
2. Garnish with the cilantro and serve with corn chips or as a topping for a salad or a bean dish.

GARLIC CROUTONS

What's a salad without croutons? Making your own is a great way to use up stale bread.

YIELD: ABOUT 4 CUPS

4 cups whole-grain bread, cut into 1/2-inch cubes

3 tablespoons olive oil

4 cloves garlic, pressed

1/4 teaspoon sea salt, or to taste

1. Place the bread cubes in a medium-size mixing bowl. In a separate bowl, combine the oil, garlic, and salt. Drizzle the garlic oil over the bread cubes and toss to coat well.
2. Arrange the bread cubes in a single layer on a baking sheet and bake in a preheated 350°F oven for 15 minutes, or until the cubes are crisp. Allow to cool, then serve on salads or in soups. Store any leftover croutons in a plastic bag in the freezer.

TUNISIAN EGGPLANT SALAD

Yield: 6–8 servings

- 1 large eggplant
- 1 medium tomato, finely chopped
- ½ green bell pepper, finely chopped
- ¼ cup minced fresh parsley
- 1 tablespoon olive oil
- 1 tablespoon lemon juice or white wine vinegar
- 3 cloves garlic, pressed
- ½ teaspoon ground cumin
- ½ teaspoon sea salt
- ½ teaspoon harissa (optional)*
- Cilantro leaves for garnish

In Tunisian restaurants, as soon as you sit down, you are served plates of assorted olives, baskets of French bread, and little bowls of harissa hot-pepper paste. You can then visit the buffet, where you will find a selection of salads, including one very similar to this one.

1. Pierce the eggplant all over with a fork. Place the eggplant on a baking sheet and bake in a preheated 400°F oven for about 40 minutes, or until soft and shriveled. Set aside to cool.
2. When the eggplant is cool enough to handle, scoop out the flesh and discard the skin. Chop or mash the eggplant into small pieces and place in a medium-size bowl. Add the remaining ingredients and mix well.
3. Garnish with cilantro and serve as an appetizer with Sesame, Poppy Seed, and Garlic Pita Points (page 145), or heap onto a bed of salad greens topped with feta.

*Harissa is a fiery hot sauce made with chiles. It is from Tunisia and can be purchased at Middle Eastern food stores.

SIDE DISHES

Garlic and vegetables are perfect mates. They are both incredibly good for you, and garlic makes anything that is good a little better. Even people who claim not to like certain vegetables can be tempted to partake when the dish is prepared with garlic.

WINTER SQUASH WITH GARLIC AND MISO

YIELD: 4–6 SERVINGS

1¾-pound winter squash, such as butternut, hubbard, turban, delicata, or red kuri

1 teaspoon white or yellow miso, or to taste

1 clove garlic, pressed, or to taste

This is a colorful side dish that will brighten up any ordinary meal. If you don't care for squash cooked with cinnamon and sugar, try it like this. It is savory and luscious.

1. Wash the squash and, with a knife, pierce it in a few places. Place the squash on a baking sheet and bake in a preheated 350°F oven for about 45 minutes, or until tender. When it is done, a knife or fork can be easily inserted into the flesh. Set aside to cool.
2. When the squash is cool enough to handle, cut it in half and scoop out the seeds and stringy parts. Scrape the flesh from the skin and place in a bowl. Discard the skin. Add the miso and mash the squash. Add the garlic and mix well. Serve warm.

PATTY PAN SQUASH WITH RED PEPPERS

YIELD: 4 SERVINGS

1–2 tablespoons olive oil
1 cup sliced red onion
4 cloves garlic, minced
1 teaspoon dried basil
1 1/4 pounds patty pan squash, cut into 1/4-inch slices, then halved
1 red bell pepper, sliced
1 tablespoon balsamic vinegar
1 tablespoon tamari soy sauce

This is a colorful and very Italian tasting dish. It is a wonderful accompaniment to Polenta-Stuffed Portabella Mushrooms (page 176).

1. Heat the oil in a large skillet. Add the onion and sauté for 1 minute. Add the garlic and basil, and sauté for another minute.
2. Add the squash and the peppers, and stir to combine. Cover and cook over medium-high heat for 3 minutes more, or until the vegetables are very hot and starting to sizzle. Stir the mixture and add the vinegar and tamari, then cover quickly so the vegetables can steam. Cook, stirring occasionally, for about 5 minutes more, or until the vegetables are tender. Serve hot.

VARIATION

If you cannot find patty pan squash, use yellow summer squash.

BROILED BELGIAN ENDIVES

YIELD: 2 SERVINGS

2 Belgian endives
2 teaspoons olive oil
2 teaspoons tamari soy sauce
2 cloves garlic, pressed
1 teaspoon minced fresh tarragon, or 2 teaspoons minced garlic chives

The mild flavor and crispy texture of Belgian endives are delectably enlivened with pressed garlic.

1. Clean the endives, removing any damaged outer leaves, and cut them in half lengthwise. Place cut-side up on an oiled baking sheet.
2. Combine the oil, tamari, and garlic in a cup or small bowl. Drizzle over the endives.
3. Place the endives under a preheated broiler for about 3 minutes, or until the tops start to brown. Turn over and broil for another 2–3 minutes, or until the other sides start to brown. Sprinkle with the tarragon or garlic chives and serve immediately.

GARLIC BROILED TOMATOES

Spice up a summer meal with these broiled tomatoes.

1. Remove the core and a thin slice from the top and bottom of each tomato and discard. Cut the tomatoes into slices 1/2–3/4 inch thick and place on a lightly oiled baking sheet.
2. Combine the oil and garlic in a cup or small bowl and brush on the tomato slices. Sprinkle with salt, if desired.
3. Place the tomatoes under a preheated broiler for about 3–5 minutes, or until they are hot and bubbly. Be careful not to overcook. Garnish with basil and oregano, and serve immediately.

YIELD: 4 SERVINGS

4 medium tomatoes

1 tablespoon olive oil

4 cloves garlic, pressed

Sea salt to taste (optional)

Chopped fresh basil for garnish

Chopped fresh oregano for garnish

STUFFED MUSHROOMS

This recipe makes an attractive appetizer or vegetable side dish.

1. Wash the mushrooms and carefully remove their stems. Mince the stems and place in a medium-size bowl along with the bread crumbs, garlic, tamari, rosemary, and white pepper. Mix well. Stuff the mixture into the mushroom caps, mounding it slightly.
2. Place the filled mushroom caps on a lightly oiled baking sheet. Cover the mushrooms tent-style with aluminum foil (don't let the foil touch the mushrooms) and bake in a preheated 350°F oven for 20 minutes. Uncover and bake for 10 minutes more. Sprinkle with the parsley and serve immediately.

*To make bread crumbs, tear two slices of whole-grain bread into pieces, place in a blender or food processor, and process into fine crumbs. Freeze any leftover crumbs.

YIELD: 24 STUFFED MUSHROOMS

24 medium-size button or crimini mushrooms

1 cup whole-grain bread crumbs, lightly packed*

10 cloves garlic, pressed

1 tablespoon plus 1 teaspoon tamari soy sauce

1/2 tablespoon minced fresh rosemary

1/4 teaspoon white pepper

Minced fresh parsley for garnish

GARLIC ROASTED POTATOES

YIELD: 4 SERVINGS

2½ pounds potatoes (new, sweet, or combination of both)

12 cloves garlic, cut into halves

2 tablespoons olive oil

1 teaspoon sea salt

1 large Vidalia onion, cut into thick slices (optional)

1 heaping tablespoon curry powder, or 2 tablespoons minced fresh rosemary

There are many variations to this recipe. You can make it with both new potatoes and sweet potatoes, or a combination of both. Whether you season the potatoes with curry powder or rosemary also makes a big difference, but any way you make them, there is never enough.

1. Scrub the potatoes and cut them into bite-size chunks. If you use a combination of new and sweet potatoes, cut the sweet potatoes into slightly larger chunks because they cook a little faster.
2. Place the potato chunks in a large bowl along with the garlic, oil, and salt. Add the onion, if desired, and either the curry powder or the rosemary. Mix well.
3. Turn the mixture onto a large cookie sheet and spread into an even layer. Bake in a preheated 350°F oven for 50 minutes, or until the potatoes are tender and browned. Serve immediately.

MASHED POTATOES WITH ROASTED GARLIC AND HERBS

This is a recipe that all garlic lovers will adore. Feel free to vary the seasoning ingredients to suit your taste. Any way you prepare these potatoes, they're scrumptious.

YIELD: ENOUGH FOR 4 POLITE PEOPLE OR 2 SHAMELESS GOURMANDS

- 2 bulbs garlic
- 1 teaspoon olive oil
- 2 pounds potatoes (mealy old baking potatoes are fine)
- 2–3 cups water
- 2 tablespoons flax oil or butter
- 1/4 cup potato water or milk
- 1/4 cup chopped fresh parsley or garlic chives
- 1 1/2 teaspoons finely chopped fresh rosemary (optional)
- 1/2 teaspoon sea salt, or to taste
- 1/4 teaspoon white pepper, or to taste

1. Separate the garlic cloves from the bulbs, leaving the clove wrappers intact. Place in a small oven-proof dish, drizzle with the oil, and toss to coat. Cover with aluminum foil and bake in a preheated 350°F oven for about 30 minutes, or until soft and mushy. Set aside until cool enough to handle.
2. Scrub the potatoes and cut out any eyes or discolorations. Peel if not organic or if the skins are too thick, and place in a medium-size saucepan with the water.* Bring to a boil, then reduce the heat and cook for about 20 minutes, or until tender. Add more water if necessary.
3. While the potatoes are cooking, remove the garlic cloves from their wrappers. To do this, pierce the wrappers with a paring knife and then squeeze out the roasted cloves. Set aside.
4. When the potatoes are tender, drain them, reserving the cooking water, and place in a large bowl. Mash, along with the flax oil, potato water, parsley, and rosemary, if desired.
5. Stir in the garlic, salt, and pepper, and serve immediately.

*It is not necessary to completely cover the potatoes with water to cook them. If you completely cover them, you will not only lose a lot of healthy minerals, but the potatoes will take longer to cook. I either pressure-cook my potatoes using about 1 1/2 cups of water or cook them in waterless cookware using just 1–2 tablespoons of water. In a conventional pan, you will need about 2–3 cups of water. I usually then mash any remaining cooking water into the potatoes. If you have more than enough cooking water remaining, put the leftover water into a freezer container and freeze for future use in soup stocks.

ROASTED GARLIC POTATO CAKES

If you ever find yourself with leftover Mashed Potatoes with Roasted Garlic and Herbs, try this recipe—it's my favorite way to use them up. In fact, I love this recipe so much that I often make extra mashed potatoes. These potato cakes are delicious with eggs for Sunday brunch or as a vegetable side dish with just about anything.

Cold leftover Mashed Potatoes with Roasted Garlic and Herbs (page 161)

Whole-wheat pastry flour as needed

Olive oil as needed

1. Shape the leftover mashed potatoes into little patties and dredge the patties in the flour, coating both sides.
2. Heat a small amount of oil in a skillet and cook the patties over medium heat until browned on both sides. Serve immediately.

BAKED GARLICKY PARSNIPS

Parsnips are a good vegetable to use in the winter. This recipe takes up very little room in the oven, so you may wish to make it when you are baking something else.

YIELD: 2–4 SERVINGS

3 cups sliced parsnips (about 4–8 small)

1–2 tablespoons olive oil

6 cloves garlic, minced

2 tablespoons minced fresh parsley

Pinch nutmeg

Pinch sea salt

1. Place the parsnips in a baking dish and drizzle with the oil. Add the garlic and mix. Cover and bake, stirring once or twice, in a preheated 350°F oven for about 30 minutes, or until the parsnips are tender.
2. Uncover and broil for 2 minutes, or until parsnips are lightly browned.
3. Add the parsley and toss to coat. Sprinkle with the nutmeg and salt, and serve immediately.

GARLIC-PARMESAN RICE CAKES

In addition to enjoying these crisp little patties as a side dish, I sometimes top them with a savory spread like White Bean Purée (page 133) and surround them in a sea of Luscious Tomato-Garlic Sauce (page 152) for an elegant vegetarian entrée.

YIELD: 6 PATTIES

- 1½ cups short-grain brown rice
- 3 cups water
- ½ cup freshly grated Parmesan cheese
- 3–4 cloves garlic, pressed
- ½ teaspoon celery seeds
- ½ teaspoon sea salt
- 1–2 tablespoons olive oil

1. Place the rice in a medium-size saucepan. Cover with water, swish around to wash, then drain using a wire strainer. Return the rice to the pan and add the 3 cups water. Cover and bring to a boil over high heat, then reduce the heat to medium-low and simmer, without stirring, for about 45 minutes, or until the water is absorbed. Transfer the cooked rice to a large bowl and set aside until just cool enough to handle. Do not chill.
2. When the rice has cooled, add the Parmesan cheese, garlic, celery seeds, and salt. Mix well using your hands and shape into 6 patties.
3. Heat the oil in a skillet and cook the patties over medium heat for about 3 minutes on each side, or until crispy brown.
4. Serve plain or topped with a dollop of your favorite spread.

ENTRÉES

What could be more satisfying than a meal revolving around a savory garlicky entrée that is as healthy as it is scrumptious? Here you will find some recipes for fish and poultry dishes, along with several delectable meatless entrées. Whole grains, such as brown rice, quinoa, polenta, and whole-grain pasta, make a wonderful bed for saucy garlic dishes. They are truly worth discovering if they are not already a part of your culinary repertoire.

GARLICKY ORANGE–POPPY SEED CHICKEN

Easy to make and full of flavor. Try it with Mashed Potatoes with Roasted Garlic and Herbs (page 161) and a green salad.

YIELD: 4 SERVINGS

- 4 skinless, boneless chicken breasts, flattened
- Juice from 2 oranges
- 2 tablespoons grated orange peel
- 2 cups whole-wheat bread crumbs*
- 2 tablespoons poppy seeds
- 2 teaspoons ground cumin
- 6 cloves garlic, pressed
- Cayenne pepper to taste
- Sea salt to taste
- 1 cup whole-wheat pastry flour

1. Rinse the chicken and pat dry. Place in a shallow bowl with the orange juice and marinate in the refrigerator for 1–2 hours. (The acids in the juice will tenderize the chicken.)
2. In a shallow dish, combine the orange peel with the bread crumbs, poppy seeds, cumin, garlic, cayenne, and salt. Place the flour in a separate shallow dish. Dredge the chicken in the flour, shaking off the excess. Then dip in the orange juice marinade and roll in the bread crumb mixture. Place in a lightly oiled 9-x-13-inch baking dish, cover tightly with aluminum foil, and bake in a preheated 450°F oven for 15 minutes.
3. Reduce the heat to 350°F. Remove the foil, turn the chicken pieces over, and bake, uncovered, for 20 minutes more, or until the chicken is tender and the juices run clear when pierced with a fork. Serve hot.

*To make bread crumbs, tear four slices of whole-grain bread into pieces, place in a blender or food processor, and process into fine crumbs. Freeze any leftover crumbs.

STEPHEN'S GARLIC-HERB BAKED CHICKEN

This recipe is from my neighbor Stephen Plotkin. He has the largest cookbook collection of anyone I know, but when he cooks, he keeps it simple. In this recipe, the whole chicken becomes infused with the scent of fresh herbs and garlic.

Yield: 4 servings

- 4-pound chicken
- Cloves from 1 garlic bulb, peeled
- Fresh oregano or rosemary to taste

1. Rinse the chicken and pat dry. Stuff the cavity with the garlic and as much rosemary or oregano as you can fit.
2. Place the chicken in a roasting pan and tent with a piece of aluminum foil. Bake in a preheated 300°F oven for about 4 hours, or until the juices run clear. Serve with brown basmati rice, sautéed vegetables, and a green salad.

GARLIC AND SAGE TURKEY BURGERS

Don't reserve the winning combination of turkey and sage for Thanksgiving. It marries beautifully with garlic in these gourmet burgers.

Yield: 4 servings

- 1 pound ground turkey
- 1 tablespoon finely minced fresh sage, or 1/2 teaspoon dried
- 4 cloves garlic, pressed
- 1/2 teaspoon sea salt, or to taste
- 1/4 teaspoon white pepper
- 1–2 tablespoons olive oil
- 1 tablespoon lemon juice
- 4 whole-grain buns, toasted
- 4 tomato slices
- 4 lettuce leaves

1. Place the ground turkey, sage, garlic, salt, and white pepper in a large bowl and mix well. Shape into 4 patties. Cover and refrigerate for 30 minutes to blend the flavors.
2. Heat the oil in a nonstick skillet and cook the patties for about 3–4 minutes, or until they are firm and dark brown on top. Flip and cook about 3–4 minutes more, or until cooked all the way through. Sprinkle with lemon juice and serve each burger on a toasted bun with a tomato slice and lettuce leaf.

CHICKEN PROVENÇAL (40-CLOVE CHICKEN)

YIELD: 4 SERVINGS

4-pound chicken, cut into pieces

Sea salt and pepper to taste

3 tablespoons olive oil

40 cloves garlic, unpeeled, with a thin slice cut off the bottom end of each clove

1 lemon, seeded and cut into paper-thin slices

4 stalks celery, chopped

3/4 cup dry white wine

2 teaspoons herbes de Provence

1/4 cup minced Italian parsley

Most American recipes for 40-Clove Chicken call for peeling the garlic before putting it into the pan. The French, however, leave it unpeeled and let their guests squeeze the garlic out of its skin and onto bread provided at the table. I prefer the French way—it is less work for the cook.

1. Sprinkle the chicken pieces with salt and pepper, and rub into the skin.
2. Heat the oil in a large skillet and cook the chicken pieces until lightly browned on all sides.
3. Place the garlic cloves in a single layer in the bottom of a 9-x-13-inch baking dish, then arrange the chicken pieces, skin side up, on top of the garlic. Layer the lemon slices over the chicken, then sprinkle the celery on top of the lemon and pour on the wine. Sprinkle with herbs de Provence and parsley. Cover and bake in a preheated 375°F oven for 1 1/2 hours or until the chichen is tender and completely cooked.
4. Serve with French country-style bread, a steamed veggie, and an enormous salad.

THE ARTIST'S POACHED CHICKEN

This recipe comes from my dear friend Louise Hamel, who is a fabulous artist as well as a great cook. I usually enjoy this dish with eggplant, zucchini, and bell peppers that are sautéed with garlic oil.

YIELD: 4 SERVINGS

2 skinless, boneless chicken breast halves

16 cloves garlic, roasted and mashed

1 cup water

1 onion, sliced

1 stalk celery, chopped

1 teaspoon whole peppercorns

1 teaspoon herbes de Provence

2 bay leaves

1 tablespoon lemon juice

2 teaspoons butter

2 teaspoons capers

1/4 teaspoon sea salt, or to taste

1. Make a slice into the thickest part of each chicken breast to form a pocket. Stuff each pocket with one-fourth of the garlic.
2. Combine the water, onion, celery, peppercorns, herbes de Provence, and bay leaves in a large saucepan. Add the chicken, bring the liquid to a boil, then reduce the heat to medium-low and simmer, covered, for 10–12 minutes, or until the chicken is cooked through.
3. Remove the chicken from the pan and set aside. Add the lemon juice, butter, capers, and salt to the liquid in the pan and simmer for 1 minute.
4. To serve, arrange the chicken on a serving platter and top with the lemon-butter mixture.

LOUISE'S GARLIC-MARINATED GRILLED SALMON

This is another recipe from my friend Louise Hamel.

Yield: 4 servings

- 1/4 cup water
- 2 tablespoons tamari soy sauce
- 2 tablespoons olive oil
- 1 tablespoon Worcestershire sauce
- 1 tablespoon maple syrup
- 6 cloves garlic, pressed
- 2-pound salmon filet

1. In a small saucepan, mix together the water, tamari, oil, Worcestershire sauce, maple syrup, and garlic. Bring to a boil, then reduce the heat and simmer for 5–10 minutes, or until reduced to 1/4 cup. Set aside and let cool to room temperature.
2. Place the salmon in a shallow dish, cover with the marinade, and let sit for 30 minutes.
3. Cook the salmon 3 minutes per side on a gas grill. Do not overcook or it will dry out. Serve with brown jasmine rice and a salad.

EASY SHRIMP IN GARLIC-WINE SAUCE

This quick recipe will appeal to both seafood lovers and garlic lovers.

Yield: 4–6 servings

- 2 tablespoons olive oil
- 12 cloves garlic, minced
- 1 pound shrimp, peeled and deveined
- 1/3 cup white wine
- 1/4 cup chopped scallions
- 2 tablespoons lemon juice
- Hot sauce to taste
- 2 tablespoons minced fresh garlic grass or chives
- 2 tablespoons minced fresh parsley

1. Heat the oil in a wok or large skillet over high heat. Add the garlic and cook for a few seconds. Add the shrimp and cook, stirring continually, for 2 minutes more. Add the wine, scallions, lemon juice, and hot sauce, and cook for another 3 minutes, or just until the shrimp are slightly pink or opaque. (Be careful not to overcook the shrimp or they will become tough.)
2. Arrange the shrimp over brown rice or whole-grain noodles and sprinkle with garlic grass and parsley. Serve with a green salad.

RED LENTIL LOAF

This recipe makes an easy and tasty meatless main course. I usually serve it topped with Lucious Tomato-Garlic Sauce (page 152).

YIELD: 4 SERVINGS

1 cup dry red lentils
2 cups water
1 cup cooked brown rice
1 cup oat flakes
1 cup grated carrot
2 scallions, chopped
1/4 cup bread crumbs*
1 egg, beaten, or egg replacer to equal 1 egg
3 tablespoons tamari soy sauce
6 cloves garlic, pressed
1 teaspoon dried sage

1. Pick through the lentils to remove any dirt, stones, or damaged legumes, then wash and drain. Place in a large pot with the water, and cover. Bring to a boil, then reduce the heat and simmer, stirring occasionally, for about 15 minutes, or until the water is absorbed.
2. While the lentils are cooking, mix together the rice, oat flakes, carrot, scallions, bread crumbs, egg, tamari, garlic, and sage in a large bowl.
3. Add the cooked lentils to the rice-oat mixture and mix well.
4. Oil a 4-x-8-x-2-inch loaf pan and sprinkle the sides and bottom with oat flakes to keep the loaf from sticking. Pack the loaf mixture into the pan and bake in a preheated 350°F oven for 40 minutes.
5. Remove from the oven and let stand 5–10 minutes. Run a knife around the edge of the loaf and remove it from the pan onto a serving platter. Serve with a green salad.

*To make bread crumbs, tear a slice of whole-grain bread into pieces, place in a blender or food processor, and process into fine crumbs. Freeze any leftover crumbs.

YIELD: 4 SERVINGS

4 sturdy branches of fresh rosemary

24 shrimp, shelled and deveined

1/4 cup tamari soy sauce

1/4 cup fresh lemon juice

2 tablespoons olive oil

4 cloves garlic, pressed

GRILLED ROSEMARY-SKEWERED GARLIC-MARINATED SHRIMP

Freshly cut rosemary branches make perfect skewers for marinated shrimp, infusing them with flavor as they grill.

1. Strip the leaves off the rosemary branches and save for future use. Thread 6 shrimp onto each rosemary skewer and place in a shallow dish.
2. Combine the tamari, lemon juice, oil, and garlic in a cup or small bowl. Pour over the shrimp and marinate for 30 minutes, turning once.
3. Cook the shrimp over a gas grill for 3 minutes on each side, or until the shrimp are pink. Serve with lemon wedges.

GINGER-GARLIC TOFU

This tofu is a great addition to any vegetable stir-fry. You may want to double the recipe to create leftovers.

YIELD: 2–3 SERVINGS

1 pound firm tofu

2 tablespoons tamari soy sauce, or to taste

1 tablespoon finely grated ginger

1 teaspoon toasted sesame oil

6 cloves garlic

1 tablespoon plus 1 teaspoon arrowroot powder

1. Slice the tofu into small rectangles or cubes and arrange in a single layer in a shallow dish.
2. Combine the tamari, ginger, oil, and garlic in a cup or small bowl. Add enough water to just cover and stir to mix. Pour over the tofu and let marinate at least 30 minutes. The longer it marinates, the better. You can also place the tofu in the refrigerator and marinate for several hours or overnight.
3. Reserving the liquid, remove the tofu and place on a well-oiled cookie sheet. Bake in a preheated 375°F oven for 35–40 minutes, or until the desired crispness is reached. The longer the tofu bakes, the firmer and crispier it will become. However, if it bakes too long, it will become tough.
4. To make the sauce, mix the arrowroot into the reserved marinade. Place in a small saucepan and bring to a boil. Remove from the heat, add the tofu, and stir carefully to coat.
5. Serve over a bed of rice or pasta, accompanied by steamed or stir-fried vegetables. You can also add this tofu to another recipe, such as a vegetable stew.

PINTO BEANS À MA FAÇON

YIELD: 4–6 SERVINGS

1 pound dry pinto beans

3 tablespoons tamari soy sauce

1 tablespoon balsamic vinegar

6 bay leaves

20 sun-dried tomato halves, cut into pieces with scissors

1 onion, chopped

3 cloves garlic, pressed, or to taste

This is my version of a Southern and soul-food favorite.

1. Pick through the beans to remove any dirt, stones, or damaged beans, then wash and drain. Place the beans in a large bowl and add enough water to cover by approximately 2 inches. Soak for 8–10 hours. Drain and rinse.
2. Place the beans in a large, heavy kettle such as a cast-iron Dutch oven and add enough water to cover by approximately 2 inches. Cover and bring to a boil over high heat. Reduce the heat to low and gently simmer, stirring occasionally, for 1 hour.
3. Add the tamari, vinegar, bay leaves, tomatoes, and onion, and simmer for 1 hour more, or until the beans are very tender and the mixture has thickened. Add more water as needed. Remove the beans from the heat and add the garlic.
4. Garnish with finely chopped fresh herbs such as parsley, cilantro, garlic chives, or basil. Serve as is alongside sliced tomatoes and cornbread, or over rice, millet, or polenta.

VARIATIONS

Stir cumin and cayenne pepper to taste into the beans and garnish with fresh cilantro and salsa for a Mexican-style dish. Serve with corn tortillas, avocado, and a green salad.

BLACK BEAN–STUFFED YELLOW PEPPERS

I love the way this dish looks with yellow peppers, but you can also use green or red varieties, or a mixture of all three.

Yield: 4–8 servings

- 4 large bell peppers
- 1 tablespoon olive oil
- 1 cup chopped onion
- 6 cloves garlic, sliced
- 1 tablespoon chili powder
- 1 teaspoon ground cumin
- 1 teaspoon dried basil
- 1/2 teaspoon dried oregano
- 2 cups cooked and drained black beans
- 1 tablespoon balsamic vinegar
- 2 1/2 cups cooked brown rice
- 1 cup chopped tomato
- 1 teaspoon sea salt
- 8 slices Monterey Jack cheese (optional)

1. Cut the peppers in half lengthwise and remove the seeds. Place the halves cut side down on a steamer rack set in a large pan. Add about 1/2 inch of water to the pan, cover, and bring to a boil. Reduce the heat and steam the peppers for 5 minutes, or until nearly tender but still holding their shape well. Remove from the heat and set aside.
2. Heat the oil in a skillet over medium heat. Add the onion and sauté until nearly tender. Add the garlic, chili powder, cumin, basil, and oregano, and continue to sauté until the onion is tender. Add the beans and vinegar, mix well, then stir in the rice, tomato, and salt.
3. Fill the pepper halves with the bean mixture. Top each with a slice of cheese, if desired, and place in a shallow baking dish. Bake, covered, in a preheated 350°F oven for about 15–20 minutes, or until the peppers are tender. Serve with salsa and a big green salad.

SIMPLE SPRINGTIME PASTA

YIELD: 4 SERVINGS

1 pound asparagus, cut into 1-inch pieces

10 ounces whole-grain pasta

2 tablespoons olive oil

2–3 garlic scallions, chopped, or 4–6 garlic cloves, minced

2–3 tablespoons water

Sea salt to taste

Freshly ground black pepper to taste

Freshly grated Parmesan cheese (optional)

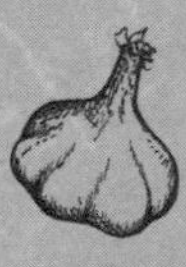

Fresh asparagus in the garden is always a welcome sign that summer's bounty will soon arrive; garlic scallions are a reminder that a new crop of garlic is on the way.

1. Bring a large pot of water to a rolling boil. Add the pasta and cook according to package directions.
2. While the pasta cooks, heat the oil in a large skillet over medium heat. Add the garlic scallions, and sauté 1 minute. Stir in the asparagus, cover, and cook 2 minutes more. Add the water, quickly cover, and steam for 2–3 minutes, or until the asparagus is tender. Remove from the heat, add the salt and pepper, and stir the ingredients to combine.
3. Reserving about 1/4 cup of the cooking water, drain the pasta and transfer to a warmed bowl. Add the asparagus mixture and toss. If the mixture appears dry, add the cooking water 1 tablespoon at a time until the desired consistency is reached.
4. Sprinkle with cheese, if desired, and serve immediately.

LAZY GUY'S PASTA WITH TOMATOES AND GARLIC

This is another one of those simple recipes that depend on having super high quality ingredients and fresh vine-ripened tomatoes.

Yield: 4 servings

10 ounces whole-grain pasta

4 medium ripe tomatoes

3 tablespoons chopped fresh basil

3 tablespoons minced fresh Italian parsley

2–3 tablespoons tamari soy sauce

2 tablespoons olive oil

1–2 tablespoons balsamic vinegar, or to taste

3–4 cloves garlic, pressed

Freshly ground pepper to taste

1. Bring a large pot of water to a rolling boil. Add the pasta and cook according to package directions.
2. While the pasta cooks, finely chop the tomatoes and place in a large bowl. Add the basil, parsley, tamari, oil, vinegar, garlic, and pepper, and mix well.
3. Drain the pasta and add to the bowl with the tomato mixture. Toss to coat.
4. Serve as is or topped with freshly grated Parmesan cheese or some fresh chevrè.

VARIATION

Top the pasta with sautéed broccoli or spinach, along with a handful of walnuts. Or add some crumbled feta cheese. Decrease or omit the tamari if adding feta.

POLENTA-STUFFED PORTABELLA MUSHROOMS

YIELD: 2 SERVINGS

Polenta

1/2 cup cornmeal

2 cups water

1/4 teaspoon sea salt

Mushrooms

2 large portabella mushrooms, stems removed

1 tablespoon olive oil

6 cloves garlic, pressed

1 teaspoon dried thyme

1/4 teaspoon sea salt

1/4 cup freshly grated Parmesan cheese

Minced fresh parsley, or chopped fresh garlic chives for garnish

When my husband is in Rome, his home away from home is Il Margutta Vegetariano, a trendy vegetarian restaurant that has fabulous décor and a beautiful clientele. This recipe is not from there, but it tastes like it could be.

1. To make the polenta, combine the cornmeal, water, and salt in a heavy, medium-sized saucepan. Stirring constantly, bring the mixture to a boil, then reduce the heat to low and cook, stirring often, for about 20 minutes, or until the polenta becomes very thick. If the mixture starts to splatter when it begins to boil, cover the pan for 3–4 minutes, then remove the lid, stir, and continue to cook, uncovered, over low heat.
2. While the polenta is cooking, preheat the broiler. Place the oil in a cup or small bowl and brush some over the tops of the mushrooms. Place the mushrooms cap side down on a cookie sheet.
3. Add the garlic, thyme, and 1/4 teaspoon salt to the remaining oil, stir, and brush over the stem sides of the mushrooms. Place the mushrooms on the top rack of the oven, and broil for 5 minutes. Reduce the heat to 475°F and move the mushrooms to the bottom rack for 5 minutes more, or until they are cooked through.
4. Fill the mushroom caps with polenta, sprinkle with cheese, and place under the broiler for 3 minutes, or until the cheese is bubbly and lightly browned.
5. To serve, center each mushroom on individual plates, and garnish with parsley.

GRANDMA'S OATMEAL BURGERS

This is one of my oldest recipes, which resurfaced after it was printed in a local magazine. I think of these burgers as vegetarian comfort food because they are so rich and meaty tasting.

YIELD: 4 SERVINGS

1 cup regular rolled oats (not instant or quick-cooking oats)

3 eggs

3/4 cup freshly grated sharp cheddar cheese

1/4 cup sesame seeds

1/4 cup finely minced onion

2 tablespoons tamari soy sauce

4 cloves garlic, pressed

1/2 teaspoon dried sage

1–2 tablespoons olive oil

1 cup sliced mushrooms

Sauce

3/4 cup tomato juice

3/4 cup water

2 1/2 tablespoons whole-wheat pastry flour

1 tablespoon tamari soy sauce

1. Place the oats, eggs, cheese, sesame seeds, onion, tamari, garlic, and sage in a large bowl and mix well.
2. Heat the oil in a large skillet. Using a spoon, divide the oatmeal mixture into fourths and carefully drop into the skillet. Cook over medium heat for 4 minutes, or until browned on the bottom. Flip and continue to cook until the other side is browned. (Note that the patties will not stick together until they begin to cook, so they cannot be shaped into burgers beforehand.)
3. While the burgers cook, combine the sauce ingredients in a small bowl. Mix well to remove any floury lumps.
4. Arrange the mushrooms on the burgers, then top with the sauce. Cover and simmer for 5 minutes.
5. Serve with ears of fresh corn-on-the-cob, ripe tomatoes, and steamed green beans for a delicious American-style meal.

VEGETABLE POT-AU-FEU (BAKED VEGETABLE STEW)

YIELD: 4 SERVINGS

1 large baking potato
1 large sweet potato
1 small rutabaga, or 2 medium white turnips
2 large carrots
1 medium parsnip
3½ cups chopped onion
2 cups water or vegetable stock
¼ cup tamari soy sauce
12 cloves garlic, halved
5 bay leaves

Sauce

2 tablespoons olive oil
4 tablespoons whole-wheat pastry flour
1 teaspoon curry powder
1 teaspoon dried tarragon
⅓ cup water

This garlicky root-vegetable stew is the perfect warming meal for a cold winter's evening.

1. Cut the potatoes, rutabaga, carrots, and parsnip into medium-size chunks and place in a large, deep baking dish along with the onion, water, tamari, garlic, and bay leaves. Cover and bake in a preheated 350°F oven for about 1½ hours, or until the vegetables are tender.
2. When the vegetables are almost tender, prepare the sauce. Heat the oil in a small saucepan. Add the flour, curry powder, and tarragon, and stir to combine. Cook, stirring constantly, over medium-high heat for about 3–4 minutes, or until the flour browns and begins to give off a nutty aroma. Remove from the heat and add the water, stirring vigorously to form a smooth paste.
3. Add the flour mixture to the vegetables and mix well to thicken the stew. If too thin, bake the stew uncovered for 5 minutes, or until it thickens. If too thick, add a little water.
4. Serve hot along with a crisp green salad and some fresh whole-grain sourdough bread.

Conclusion

From primitive cave dwellers to urbanites in glass high-rises, humans throughout the ages have shared my fascination with garlic. As an object of both love and disdain, garlic has had the power to attract, repulse, and serve humanity from time immemorial. The process of writing this book has allowed my love for garlic to flourish. As I became more familiar with garlic's history, mythology, cultivation, genealogy, and many, many uses, my love deepened into a profound respect. Garlic truly is worthy of being an object of affection.

There is an old blues song with a chorus that includes a line something like, "Don't advertise your love." Well, I may be foolish, but I am not a jealous sort of lover. It is my fondest desire to share with you the love and pleasure that I have experienced in my relationship with garlic. I hope that the mystery, lore, science, and culinary delights associated with this lowly bulb that I have presented in this book have stimulated your imagination and whetted your appetite, so that you, too, will decide to experience the gastronomic pleasures and health benefits that garlic has to offer.

Bon appetit. May all your passions be healthy ones.

Metric Conversion Tables

Common Liquid Conversions

Measurement	=	Milliliters
1/4 teaspoon	=	1.25 milliliters
1/2 teaspoon	=	2.50 milliliters
3/4 teaspoon	=	3.75 milliliters
1 teaspoon	=	5.00 milliliters
1 1/4 teaspoons	=	6.25 milliliters
1 1/2 teaspoons	=	7.50 milliliters
1 3/4 teaspoons	=	8.75 milliliters
2 teaspoons	=	10.0 milliliters
1 tablespoon	=	15.0 milliliters
2 tablespoons	=	30.0 milliliters

Measurement	=	Liters
1/4 cup	=	0.06 liters
1/2 cup	=	0.12 liters
3/4 cup	=	0.18 liters
1 cup	=	0.24 liters
1 1/4 cups	=	0.30 liters
1 1/2 cups	=	0.36 liters
2 cups	=	0.48 liters
2 1/2 cups	=	0.60 liters
3 cups	=	0.72 liters
3 1/2 cups	=	0.84 liters
4 cups	=	0.96 liters
4 1/2 cups	=	1.08 liters
5 cups	=	1.20 liters
5 1/2 cups	=	1.32 liters

Conversion Formulas

LIQUID		
When You Know	**Multiply By**	**To Determine**
teaspoons	5.0	milliliters
tablespoons	15.0	milliliters
fluid ounces	30.0	milliliters
cups	0.24	liters
pints	0.47	liters
quarts	0.95	liters

WEIGHT		
When You Know	**Multiply By**	**To Determine**
ounces	28.0	grams
pounds	0.45	kilograms

Converting Fahrenheit to Celsius

Fahrenheit	=	Celsius
200–205	=	95
220–225	=	105
245–250	=	120
275	=	135
300–305	=	150
325–330	=	165
345–350	=	175
370–375	=	190
400–405	=	205
425–430	=	220
445–450	=	230
470–475	=	245
500	=	260

Resource List

GARLIC AND GARLIC PRODUCTS

Boundary Garlic Farm
Box 273
Midway, British Columbia
Canada V0H 1M0
Phone: 250-449-2152
Website: www.garlicfarm.ca
Canadian-based company that sells organic heirloom garlic seeds.

Cayuga Garlic Farms
3176 Cork Street
Scipio Center, NY 13147
Phone: 315-364-8949
Website: www.cayugagarlic.com
Offers gourmet hardneck garlics, seed stock, and braids.

Charley's Farm
54 East Stutler Road
Spokane, WA 99224
Phone: 509-488-5374
Website: www.charleysfarm.com
Sells thirty varieties of gourmet organic garlic.

Christopher Ranch
4800 Monterey Highway
Gilroy, CA 95020
Phone: 800-537-6122
Website: www.christopher-ranch.com
Offers fresh garlic, elephant garlic, garlic braids, and a variety of garlic products including roasted cloves, pesto sauce, and pickled cloves.

Filaree Farm
182 Conconully Highway
Okanogan, WA 98840
Phone: 509-422-6940
Website: www.filareefarm.com

Has over 100 unique strains of certified-organic seed garlic from all over the world.

Garlic Festival Foods
PO Box 1145
Gilroy, CA 95021
Phone: 888-GARLICFEST
Website: www.garlicfestival.com

Sells fresh garlic and full line of garlic products, including seasonings, condiments, garlic braids, gift baskets, gadgets, and more.

Garlic Galaxy Store
1094-A1 Revere Avenue
San Francisco, CA 94124
Phone: 800-342-7542
Website: www.garlicgalaxy.com

Offers full line of garlic and garlic products, cookbooks, recipes, and gadgets.

The Garlic Gourmay
PO Box 425
Ariel, WA 98603
Phone: 866-342-7542
Website: www.garlicgourmay.com

Offers selection of garlic-mixed spices, foods, and accessories.

The Garlic Shoppe
4350 Monterey Highway
Gilroy, CA 95020
Phone: 800-842-6262
Website: www.garlicshoppe.com

This franchise has a wide array of garlic and garlic products, ranging from soups and salsas to pickles and seasonings. Also sells cookbooks, gift baskets, and lots of garlic paraphernalia. Check the website for other store locations.

The Garlic Store
Yucca Ridge Farm
46050 Weld County Road 13
Fort Collins, CO 80524
Phone: 800-854-7219
Website: www.TheGarlicStore.com

Offers "everything" garlic, including many varieties of certified-organic fresh garlic, garlicky spices, sauces, jellies, oils, and vinegars, as well as garlic books, videos, and garlic gadgets. Also, offers certified organic planting stock, organic fertilizers, and Garlic Barrier natural insect repellent.

Garlic Valley Farms
624 Ruberta Avenue
Glendale, CA 91201-2335
Phone: 800-424-7990
Website: www.garlicvalleyfarms.com

Sells cold-pressed garlic juice and roasted garlic juice. Also sells Garlic Barrier natural insect repellent.

Garlic World
4800 Monterey Highway
Gilroy, CA 95020
Phone: 800-537-6122

Website: www.garlicworld.com

A combination fruit stand, gourmet food store, and gift shop specializing in a wide variety of garlic products, including sauces, pickles, jellies, gift baskets, and books.

Giannangelo Farms Southwest
PO Box 732
Ramah, NM 87321
Phone: 505-783-4412
Website: www.avant-gardening.com

Offers workshops and a variety of instructional CDs on organic gardening.

Gourmet Garlic Gardens
12300 FM 1176
Bangs, TX 76832
Phone: 866-348-3049
Website: www.gourmetgarlicgardens.com

Has a huge selection of fresh gourmet garlics, and a variety of products including garlic-stuffed olives, pickled garlic, and garlic salsas. Also offers information on growing, preparing, preserving, and cooking with garlic.

Hawberry Farms
Providence Bay
Manitoulin Island, Ontario
Canada POP ITO
Phone: 866-427-5426
Website: www.hawberryfarms.com

Based in Ontario, Canada, this company sells a wide line of garlic products, including spreads, flakes, pastes, sauces, marinades, and gift items.

Italian Rose Garlic Products
1748-5 Australian Avenue
Riviera Beach, FL 33404
Phone: 800-338-8899
Website: www.italian-rose.com

Offers a variety of gourmet garlic dips and spreads; also sells fresh garlic and roasted garlic preserved in water.

La Terre Garlic Farm
Field Road, Box 200
Clinton Corners, NY 12514
Phone: 800-909-2272
Website: www.laterregarlic.com

Sells eight organically grown garlic varieties, as well as garlic baskets and wreaths. Offers garlic recipes on its website.

Malibu Farms Smokingarlic
1748 Colgate Drive
Thousand Oaks, CA 91360
Phone: 877-807-4706
Website: www.smokingarlic.com

Offers smoked heads of garlic, garlic seasonings, sauces, and jellies.

The Pikled Garlik Company
PO Box 543
Mesilla, NM 88046-0543
Phone: 800-775-9788
Website: www.pikledgarlik.com

Sells six flavors of pickled garlic—mild, jalapeno, red chili, lemon dill, smoke flavored, and habañero—available individually in jars or combined in wooden gift crates.

Pure Earth Organic Farm
825 Bank Street
Bridgeville, PA 15017
Website: www.pureearthorganic.com

Grows and sells certified-organic garlic, primarily Pennsylvania Extra Hearty (a Rocambole variety).

GARLIC INFORMATION WEBSITES

Garlic Central
Website: www.garlic-central.com
A free informative resource all about garlic—for cooking, health, or general interest.

Garlic Festival Foods
Website: www.garlicfestival.com
Provides garlic facts, recipes, and products.

Gourmet Garlic Gardens
Website: www.gourmetgarlicgardens.com
Garlic information center.

Wakunaga of America
Website: www.kyolic.com
Everything about aged garlic extract, with links to abstracts of scientific studies.

GARLIC FESTIVALS

United States

Delray Beach Garlic Festival
Where: Delray Beach, Florida
When: Second week in November
Phone: 561-279-0907
Website: www.dbgarlicfest.com

Fox Run's Annual Garlic Festival
Where: Seneca Lake, New York
When: First weekend in August
Phone: 800-636-9786
Website: www.foxrunvineyards.com

Gilroy Garlic Festival
Where: Gilroy, California
When: Last full weekend in July
Website: www.gilroygarlicfestival.com

Hudson Valley Garlic Festival
Where: Saugerties, New York
When: Last weekend in September
Phone: 845-246-3090
Website: www.hvgf.org

Keystone State Hot and Stinky Garlic and Herb Festival
Where: Drums, Pennsylvania
When: Last weekend in August
Website: www.zanolininursery.com/Garlicfestivals.ivnu

Pocono Garlic Festival
Where: Stroudsburg, Pennsylvania
When: First Saturday in September
Website: www.poconogarlic.com

Sunshine Hill Farm Garlic Fest
Where: Chehalis, Washington
When: Last weekend in August
Website: www.sunshinehill.net/garlicfest.htm

International

Check websites for specific festival dates.

Fête de l'Ail de Cherrueix
Where: Cherruiex, France
When: July
Website: www.feteail.jexiste.fr/

Fête de l'Ail Rose
Where: Lautrec, France
When: August
Website:
http://site.voila.fr/ailrose.lautrec/index.jhtml

Isle of Wight Garlic Festival
Where: Newchurch, England
When: August
Website:
www.wightonline.co.uk/iowgarlicfestival/

Milton's "Garlic is Great" Festival
Where: Milton, Ontario, Canada
When: August
Phone: 888-307-3276
Website: www.garlicisgreat.com

Perth Garlic Festival
Where: Perth, Ontario, Canada
When: August
Phone: 612-267-5322
Website:
www.beautifulperth.com/garlic.html

Romanian Garlic Festival
Where: Copalau, Romania
When: June
Website:
www.botosani.eu.org/garlic/index.htm

South Cariboo Garlic Festival
Where: South Cariboo, British Columbia, Canada
When: August
Website:
www.kariboofarms.com/garlic1.html

Taskopru International Garlic and Culture Festival
Where: Taskopru, Kastamonu, Turkey
When: September
Website: www.taskopru.gov.tr

Index

S

OTHER SQUAREONE TITLES OF INTEREST

GOING WILD IN THE KITCHEN

The Fresh & Sassy Tastes of Vegetarian Cooking

Leslie Cerier

Going Wild in the Kitchen is the first comprehensive global vegetarian cookbook to go beyond the standard organic beans, grains, and vegetables. In addition to providing helpful cooking tips and techniques, the book contains over 200 kitchen-tested recipes for healthful, taste-tempting dishes—creative masterpieces that contain such unique ingredients as edible flowers; sea vegetables; and wild mushrooms, berries, and herbs. It encourages the creative side of novice and seasoned cooks alike, prompting them to follow their instincts and "go wild" in the kitchen by adding, changing, or substituting ingredients in existing recipes. To help, a wealth of suggestions is found throughout. Beautiful color photographs and a list of organic foods sources complete this user-friendly cookbook.

Going Wild in the Kitchen is both a unique cookbook and a recipe for inspiration. So let yourself go! Excite your palate with this treasure-trove of unique, healthy, and taste-tempting recipe creations.

$16.95 • 224 pages • 7.5 x 9-inch quality paperback • ISBN 0-7570-0091-6

KITCHEN QUICKIES

Great, Satisfying Meals in Minutes

Marie Caratozzolo and Joanne Abrams

Ever feel that there aren't enough hours in the day to enjoy life's pleasures? Whether you're dealing with problems on the job, chasing after kids on the home front, or simply running from errand to errand, the evening probably finds you longing for a great meal, but without the time to prepare one.

Kitchen Quickies offers a solution. Virtually all of its over 170 kitchen-tested recipes—yes, really kitchen tested—call for a maximum of only five main ingredients other than kitchen staples, and each dish takes just minutes to prepare! Imagine being able to whip up dishes like Southwestern Tortilla Pizzas, Super Salmon Burgers, and Tuscan-Style Fusilli—in no time flat! As a bonus, these delicious dishes are actually good for you—low in fat and high in nutrients!

So the next time you think that there's simply no time to cook a great meal, pick up *Kitchen Quickies.* Who knows? You may even have time for a few "quickies" of your own.

$14.95 • 240 pages • 7.5 x 9-inch quality paperback • ISBN 0-7570-0085-1

Tommy Tang's Modern Thai Cuisine

Tommy Tang

Tommy Tang, celebrated chef and owner of Tommy Tang's restaurants in Los Angeles and New York, shares his flair for creating unique, delectable cuisine from his native Thailand. In *Tommy Tang's Modern Thai Cuisine,* Tommy presents over ninety of his signature recipes, which combine elements of Japanese, Indian, American, and European dishes with traditional Thai flavor. Enjoy delicacies like Thai Egg Rolls, Red Curry Shrimp, Soft Shell Crabs with Ginger-Garlic Sauce, Lemon Grass Chicken, and Tommy's special sushi. Easy-to-follow instructional illustrations guarantee professional results, while beautiful full-color photographs help you choose the perfect recipe for your next cooking adventure.

If you love Thai food, but have always thought that it was beyond your culinary reach, Tommy Tang is here to change your mind. Let *Tommy Tang's Modern Thai Cuisine* bring the joy of Thai cooking to your home.

$16.95 • 172 pages • 7.5 x 9-inch quality paperback • ISBN 0-7570-0254-4

The Sophisticated Olive

The Complete Guide to Olive Cuisine

Marie Nadine Antol

Simple, elegant, refined. With a history as old as the Bible, the humble olive has matured into a sophisticated culinary treasure. Enter any fine restaurant and you will find the sumptuous flavor of olives in cocktails, appetizers, salads, and entrées. Now, food writer Marie Nadine Antol has created *The Sophisticated Olive,* an informative guide to this glorious fruit's many healthful benefits, surprising uses, and spectacular tastes.

Part One begins by exploring the history of the olive and its range of remarkable properties, including its use as a beauty enhancer and health provider. It then goes on to describe the many olive varieties that are found throughout the world. Part Two presents over 100 kitchen-tested recipes, including salads, dressings, spreads, soups, side dishes, entrées, breads, and beverages—all designed to put a smile on the face of any olive lover.

$13.95 • 204 pages • 7.5 x 7.5-inch quality paperback • ISBN 0-7570-0024-X

Confessions of a Coffee Bean

The Complete Guide to Coffee Cuisine

Marie Nadine Antol

Our love affair with coffee continues to blossom. From coast to coast, the growing number of coffee bars serves as a testament to this romance. And now we have *Confessions of a Coffee Bean,* a complete guide to appreciating this object of our affection.

Part One of *Confessions of a Coffee Bean* opens with the history of coffee and details the coffee bean's epic journey from crop to cup. It then describes the intriguing evolution of the coffeehouse, highlights surprising facts about coffee and your health, and provides an introduction to the most enticing coffees available today. Finally, this section presents everything you need to know about making a great cup of coffee. Part Two is a tempting collection of recipes for coffee beverages, as well as desserts and treats that celebrate the very taste that is coffee.

Whether you're a true coffee aficionado or just someone who loves a good cup of java, this is a book that will entrance you with fascinating facts about all things coffee.

$13.95 • 204 pages • 7.5 x 7.5-inch quality paperback • ISBN 0-7570-0020-7

Tales of a Tea Leaf

The Complete Guide to Tea Cuisine

Jill Yates

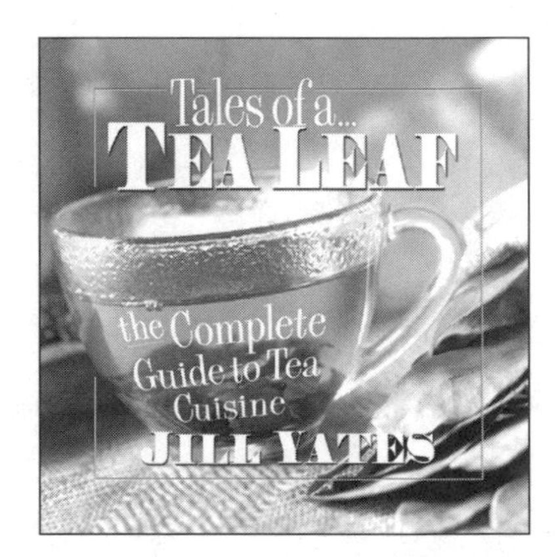

For devoted tea drinkers everywhere, *Tales of a Tea Leaf*—a complete guide to the intricacies of tea lore, tea brewing, and tea cuisine—is here.

Part One of this book begins with an exploration of the legends and lore of tea. Read through the pages to discover intriguing details of tea's regal history, including its mysterious age-old relationship with rebels and smugglers. You will also learn of the many tea types and brewing methods, as well as the remarkable health benefits of the tea leaf. Part Two presents a collection of delicious tea beverages, from refreshing iced drinks to warm, spicy brews. And because tea is so much more than an amber-colored infusion, this book also offers many other wonderful tea creations, such as Apricot Tea Bread and Pumpkin Chai Pie.

You don't need to be a tea lover to enjoy *Tales of a Tea Leaf.* With nearly 3,000 varieties steeped in almost 5,000 years of history, tea and its fascinating story can be appreciated by everyone.

$13.95 • 204 pages • 7.5 x 7.5-inch quality paperback • ISBN 0-7570-0099-1